The **Illustrated** book of

HOUSE PLANTS

The Illustrated book of
HOUSE PLANTS
Nancy Gardiner

EG EA MK ES

First published in 1998 by
New Holland Publishers (UK) Ltd
London • Cape Town • Sydney • Auckland

24 Nutford Place
London W1H 6DQ
United Kingdom

80 McKenzie Street
Cape Town 8001
South Africa

14 Aquatic Drive
Frenchs Forest, NSW 2086
Australia

MC

ISBN 1 85368 731 6 (hb)

Editor: Joy Clack
Designer: Petal Palmer
Assistant designer: Lellyn Creamer
Stylist: Sylvie Hurford
Illustrators: Erna Schoeman (page 33)
Georgina Steyn (pages 22–23, 32)

Reproduction by Hirt & Carter Cape (Pty) Ltd
Printed and bound by Times Offset (Malaysia) Sdn. Bhd.,

10 9 8 7 6 5 4 3 2

ACKNOWLEDGEMENTS

I am very grateful to Ian Glenny for making all the
terracotta pots, and to the following nurseries for the
generous loan of their plants and equipment: Celtiskloof
Nursery, McDonald's Seeds, Dunrobin Nursery,
Ray's Palms, Jungle Garden Nursery, Starke Ayres and
Rita Bowers at Greenhouse and Effects.

I would also like to express my deep gratitude to
Joy Clack and Petal Palmer for their patience and enthusiasm.

NANCY GARDINER

CONTENTS

INTRODUCTION

The Victorians had a great affinity for indoor plants. Plant collectors were sent to criss-cross the globe in search of the rare and the wonderful, and they returned with all manner of exotic beauties. There soon became a need for heating and humidity to keep these strange and beautiful plants healthy, and conservatories and elaborate glasshouses, with equally elaborate heating systems, were built to ensure their well-being.

Today these house plants are still appreciated for their beauty and natural presence, but the past intricacies of plant care have become much simpler. Cultivation expertise has improved and hybridists have created a host of new plants which are able to tolerate almost any conditions.

Air-conditioning also enables many plants, which previously would have succumbed to the adverse conditions, to survive in all climates, and offices are often seen with large containers of plants in bounding good health.

As properties diminish in size and gardens are either minimal or non-existent, householders have come to value indoor plants, delighting in the challenges involved in producing healthy specimens, whether they are luxuriant ferns or colourful African violets.

People, including the elderly and the physically disabled, who no longer have the time for gardening, have found immense pleasure and satisfaction in tending their indoor plants. Even those in hospital will often appreciate a long-lasting potted plant more than a bouquet of flowers.

Containers, too, play a role in creating the overall effect of a display of plants. On their own they can be an inherent part of the decor, but with suitable plants they add something special to any room. Today, containers are more popular than ever, and a wonderful variety can be found in garden centres, and even in interior design stores. Containers and plants can be expensive, but if they are regarded and treated as long-term investments they will prove to be good value for money.

Nurseries and garden shops have on display an enormous diversity of plants and containers, and advice is freely given, either verbally or by way of useful pamphlets.

Whether it is a miniature cactus in a tiny terracotta pot or a splendid *Ficus benjamina* in an ornate container, there is no doubt that any plant that is brought into the home will bring with it a sense of pleasure and pride as you watch it grow and flourish in your care.

CARING
FOR YOUR HOUSE PLANTS

Indoor plants are a pleasure to look after and add an air of tranquillity to any home. The plants we have in our homes today originate from all around the world and from a diversity of natural habitats. Some come from humid and shady forests, others from hot and dry desert regions. The result is a wide selection of plants, each requiring specific growing conditions. However, these plants, regardless of their natural habitat, are placed in a hot, stuffy room or in a cold, dark corner and are expected to thrive. It is surprising how many of them tolerate these adverse conditions (and it is this adaptability that makes house plants so popular), but usually only for a short time. If you learn about the plants in your home and understand where they come from, you will be able to take better care of them.

Keeping your plants in a healthy condition is not very complicated or time-consuming if you understand their basic needs. These are a suitable, fertile soil mix, sufficient moisture and food, adequate lighting and warmth, and movement of air around the plant. Hygiene is also essential when dealing with house plants. Dead flowers and leaves should be removed, pots should be kept clean, and any signs of pests or disease should be dealt with immediately.

EQUIPMENT

There is a wide selection of gardening equipment that can be used for the maintenance of house plants. Miniature tools, secateurs or scissors, spray bottles and a long-spouted watering can are the basic requirements. As both your plants and your interest in caring for them develop, your equipment can be expanded to include a range of fertilizers, moisture and temperature gauges and various plant supports.

Mist sprayer

Containers with drip saucers

String

Raffia

Fertilizer sticks

Miniature gardening tools

Watering cans

Powder fertilizers

Moisture gauge

Secateurs

Gardening gloves

Being living organisms, plants need air to survive. Together with light, air is a vital factor required for the process of photosynthesis. The quality of the air is particularly important, as stale and stagnant air will weaken the plant, whereas a good supply of fresh air will encourage healthy and luxurious growth. However, exposing plants to fresh air does not mean that they relish being in a draught – a cold blast of air will do great harm. Ensure that the air supply to the plant is gentle and at a constant temperature.

Humidity in the air is also important, especially for those plants that originated in hot and humid habitats.

To keep up humidity, particularly in hot, dry weather, spray the leaves and the air surrounding the plant with a fine mist of water. Trays of water can also be placed among the plants; if pebbles are placed in these they can make an attractive feature.

Another effective way to maintain a humid atmosphere is to use the 'pot-in-pot' method. This consists of placing a pot in a larger container, with a layer of moist soil or compost in-between. The plant will then receive a constant supply of vapour as the moisture in the outer container evaporates. Note that air-conditioning can dry out the air, causing leaves to turn brown and wilt.

Flowering plants need a strong light source and good circulation of air. Avoid placing them too close to a window as direct sunlight could burn the leaves.

All plants need light in order to produce food through a process called photosynthesis, but the intensity and duration of light a plant needs is dependent on the species. An important point to remember is that there is a significant difference between 'strong light' and 'direct sunlight'. Direct sunlight means just that – the sun's rays fall directly on the plant – whereas strong light exists in a room which is well lit by the sun but where the rays do not fall directly on the plant.

There are a number of factors to consider if you wish to achieve the best light conditions for your plant.

- Flowering plants and those with colourful or variegated leaves need more light than those with green foliage.
- Some rooms receive more natural light than others and may even receive direct sunlight. Do not place plants too close to the windows in a room with direct sunlight as their leaves could burn.
- If the inside walls and ceiling are white they will reflect more light within the room than dark colours.
- Plants that are placed in an area where there is a single light source or where the light is too weak, will grow towards the light, leading to distorted growth. This can be avoided by rotating the plant every few weeks or by moving it into a stronger light.

Plants from shady habitats, such as bromeliads and ferns, need brighter light when grown indoors. They can tolerate fairly long periods in weakly lit areas but will eventually be adversely affected by these conditions and become weak and straggly, and could even lose their colour. One of the best plants for a shady corner is the *Aspidistra*.

Special growing lights and bulbs (available from lighting stores) can be used to illuminate plants in dark corners. These can be positioned in front, behind or to the side of the plant to create an attractive lighting effect.

Some plants need filtered sunlight for healthy growth. Where the sun is too strong for these plants, Venetian blinds can lessen the intensity of the light.

Flowering plants and those with variegated or colourful foliage should be placed in a warm position with bright light. However, it may be necessary to move plants away from windows in winter as very low temperatures or frost can damage plants.

TEMPERATURE

Due to the diversity of habitats temperature control can be a tricky subject, but to ensure healthy growth house plants should be kept in conditions where the temperature remains relatively constant. The ideal temperature range is between 15 and 21 °C (60 and 70 °F) but on the whole plants are surprisingly adaptable and can tolerate fluctuations (no more than 10 °C/50 °F difference between daytime and night-time temperatures) for short periods of time. This does not apply, of course, to all plants as many will die if there is a sudden drop in temperature. However, even plants from warm climates, such as *Codiaeums* and bromeliads, have a rest period during winter and if food is cut out altogether, and watering cut down, growth will be limited and any damage caused by a sharp drop in temperature will be minimal. Keep plants away from windows during winter as glass offers no protection from the cold – move them to a warmer area of your home.

SOIL

A **good soil mixture** should provide nutrition and support to the roots, and should allow the roots and water to move freely through it, yet at the same time retain enough moisture for the plant's needs.

Note: Ordinary garden soil is not suitable for pot plants as it compacts easily and usually contains weeds, pests and diseases.

Soil is the easiest factor to manipulate and, to make it even easier, there are ready-mixed potting soils available which are suitable for most plants. These have been formulated to contain the correct amount of nutrition as well as to be of the right consistency. Also available are commercial mixes to suit particular types of plants, for example, an orchid mix or an African violet mix.

Most plants prefer a soil mix which is slightly acidic and which has good drainage. If you prefer to make up your own potting soil, you can mix sterilized loam with compost, and add coarse sand or gravel for drainage. This is the standard potting mix but most people prefer to add something extra to the soil, such as leaf mould (humus), milled bark or coarse pine-bark chips, bone meal, lime or sand, to ensure good drainage, nourishment and consistency. Superphosphate keeps the roots in good health and should always be incorporated into the soil mix – it should not be sprinkled onto the surface as it will not be able to penetrate through to the roots.

A soil mix with sufficient drainage is essential as it prevents water accumulating around the roots, which in turn leads to waterlogged conditions and the inability of the roots to take up nutrients from the soil. Charcoal, which also stops the soil from turning sour, coarse sand, vermiculite, pine-bark chips or gravel can be added to the soil to make it more friable and porous.

Many pot-plant fertilizers are available in the form of granules and tablets, which are best incorporated into the soil before planting. It is worth investigating the use of these to bring the soil into the best condition possible (see pages 20–21).

Moisture retainers (water crystals) expand to many times their size and gradually release water to the plant (they are available from nurseries and garden centres). These should also be placed into the soil at planting time, according to the manufacturer's instructions.

Too much soil can do a great deal of harm to a potted plant. If a plant is in a pot that is too big for it, the roots cannot use up the vast amount of water and food in the soil, causing the soil to turn sour and be of little use.

BASIC GUIDELINES FOR A HEALTHY PLANT

- *Don't over-water*
  Only water plants when the soil starts to dry out. The soil should be kept damp but not soggy.

- *Let your plants rest*
  Many plants need a period of dormancy at some time in the year (usually winter) to allow for strong new growth in spring. Water and food should be cut down to a minimum during this time.

- *Attend to problems immediately*
  Learn to identify the signs and symptoms of over-watering or infestation by pests or disease. If they are not treated immediately it could lead to the death of the plant or spread of the infestation to all the plants in your home.

- *Remember your plant's needs*
  Healthy, vigorous growth is achieved by maintaining optimum soil, water, temperature, light and air requirements.

Drainage stone – A layer of medium- to large-sized stones should always be placed in the base of the container to ensure good drainage. Pot liners and crocks (pieces of broken earthenware pots) are another option, as are river pebbles, which are also useful for decorating the soil in large containers.

Coarse sand – Should be added to any potting mixture to aerate and loosen the soil.

Slow-release fertilizer – This fertilizer releases its nutrients slowly into the soil.

Commercial potting soil – Pre-mixed to the right consistency and formulated to contain sufficient nutrients.

Lime – Should be added to the mix if you want to reduce acidity in the soil.

Milled bark – Has absorbent properties and retains any added water and fertilizer.

Bone meal – An organic slow-release fertilizer. 15 ml (1 tablespoon) added to a 20 cm (8 in) pot should be sufficient.

Hanging-basket mix – Usually a loose and porous mix. It is light and easy to work with but requires regular feeding.

Superphosphate – A fast-acting, inorganic fertilizer which encourages healthy root growth.

Seedling mix – Usually a soil-based mix. It is rich and fertile and has more nutrients than standard soil mixes as it contains micro-organisms which break down organic matter into essential minerals.

Gravel – A layer of gravel in the base of a small pot is an effective means of ensuring good drainage. It can also be used to decorate the surface of the soil.

Nearly every book or article that deals with house plants will make the statement that more plants are killed by over-watering than by any other cause. The delicate root hairs can take up only a certain amount of water from the soil and this is sent up through the stems to the leaves. The root hairs also need air to function properly and if the air between the soil particles is replaced with water, then the roots will soon rot and die. So, even though it is tempting to show your appreciation for your indoor plants by giving them extra water, this will only do them more harm than good.

Apart from over-watering, waterlogged conditions can also be brought about by bad drainage, often caused by clogged drainage holes in the pot. Before placing the soil in the pot, put rocks over the drainage holes, or, as some prefer, a layer of coarse sand topped with a layer of rotted leaves. Pot liners, which let the water through while retaining the soil, are available from nurseries and garden centres.

Insufficient drainage can also result when the roots find their way through the drainage holes and so block the outlet. When this happens, the plant must be potted on (see page 22).

POINTS TO REMEMBER

- Watering should be cut down during cold weather or when the plants are dormant.

- Always water plants or spray leaves early enough in the day to allow sufficient time for the leaves to dry before nightfall.

- Do not spray plants that are in the sun as the droplets can magnify the sun's rays, which could cause the leaves to burn.

- Once the roots of the plant have grown to fill the pot, it will require watering more often than one which is newly potted.

- Plants in terracotta or concrete pots will need more frequent watering than those in plastic pots, as terracotta and concrete absorb water.

- Some plants need more water than others – cacti and succulents need minimal water, whereas ferns and palms need much more.

- If a pot has been placed in an ornamental pot which is watertight, make sure there is no surplus water in the outer pot.

Good drainage is essential as over-watering can lead to the air between the soil particles being replaced with water, thus preventing the roots from absorbing the necessary nutrients for healthy growth.

To test whether a plant that has been planted in a terracotta pot needs water, gently tap the side of the pot with a small wooden mallet. A hollow sound indicates that water is needed, whereas a dull thud means that there is still plenty of water in the soil. This does not apply to plastic pots.

The best way to test for moisture is to gently dig down in the soil with your fingers – if the surface is very dry, then water is needed. With practice, you will soon come to recognize the signs that a plant needs water – even weighing a pot in your hands will let you know whether it is light enough to warrant a further watering.

The method of watering is important. A light sprinkling two or three times a week will not penetrate through the soil, with the result that the roots will grow upwards in search of water. This is not good for the roots as they are better off deep in the soil. It is best to give the pot a thorough soaking once a week, making sure that the water flows through freely. A watering can with a long, slender spout is ideal for pot plants as it can reach right into the pot. If the soil is very dry and the plant looks as though it is nearly dead, the entire pot can be dunked in a bucket of water for rapid recovery.

Spraying the leaves with a mist sprayer is highly beneficial in hot weather, but take care not to spray hairy leaves as water can accumulate around the hairs and cause the leaves to rot.

Once you have watered your plants, go back and check each one to make sure that they are not still full of water (a sign of bad drainage). Too much water can kill plants, as will too little, but somewhere in-between is a happy medium, which will keep the plants comfortably moist.

Self-watering pots, which have water in reservoirs, provide plants with a constant and sufficient supply of water. Although more expensive than conventional pots, they save a lot of time and effort.

To ensure luxurious and healthy growth, plants need nitrogen, potassium and phosphorous, which are usually found in large quantities in garden soil. Because potted plants have a limited supply of these nutrients, it is essential that they are supplemented by the addition of various organic or inorganic fertilizers.

Only established, actively growing plants with a well-developed root system should be given extra fertilizer. Plants that are dormant, newly potted, or recovering from disease should not be given extra food until the new growth is strong and healthy. Even then, the fertilizer should be at a weaker strength than normal until the plant is fully established.

How often should plants be fed? Little and often is certainly better than large doses infrequently. Fertilizers are usually accompanied by instructions as to how often the product should be applied, but once every ten to fourteen days during the plant's growing season should be sufficient.

Plants that have been bought from reliable suppliers will be growing in a fertile mixture and probably won't need supplementary feeding for at least a few weeks.

Note: Fertilizer should never be applied to dry soil. The soil should be well watered before each application, and should have a little more water added afterwards.

There is a broad range of options when it comes to choosing a fertilizer. All of them contain the essential elements and nutrients in varying quantities and come with instructions, which should be meticulously carried out – giving a plant more fertilizer than is necessary is only harmful and not kind. There are sticks, granules, powders and liquids, many of them for specific types of plants (for example, flowering or foliage plants), which makes the choice that much easier.

SLOW-RELEASE FERTILIZERS
Slow-release fertilizers gradually release small amounts of fertilizer into the soil over an extended period. They are most effective when used at the beginning of a plant's growing season as they will keep up a constant supply of

nutrients throughout the growing phase. They are available as tablets, which are coated with a substance that slowly dissolves to release the food, or as sticks (see pages 10–11), which are simply pushed into the soil. Bone meal is also an effective slow-release fertilizer.

LIQUID FERTILIZERS (FAST ACTING)

Liquid fertilizers and manure are particularly effective as they get right down to the roots immediately. They are most beneficial when used during the growing season when plants require extra nutrients for healthy production of leaves or flowers. Water-soluble powders must be dissolved in water, according to the manufacturer's instructions, before being applied to the plants.

Foliage feeding involves spraying the leaves with dissolved fertilizer, but care should be taken not to spray hairy leaves as the moisture can collect around the hairs, causing the leaves to rot. In fact, it is better to spray only a few leaves at first to make sure there is no adverse effect.

Besides these fertilizers, most of which are chemical, well-rotted manure or compost applied to the soil's surface will improve the texture and supply the plant with food.

ORGANIC VERSUS INORGANIC FERTILIZERS

In this time of ecological and environmental awareness, many people are turning to the use of organic fertilizers for gardening, and even for house-plant cultivation.

Inorganic fertilizers are made from chemicals, with the addition of nitrogen (N), phosphorous (P) and potassium (K) in varying quantities. Fertilizers with magnesium, molybdenum and other minerals are also available for plants suffering from a deficiency of these trace elements. Fertilizers have also been developed for use with specific plants such as azaleas, which require an acidic soil, and foliage plants, which need high doses of nitrogen.

Organic fertilizer is made up of organic matter and is available as compost or animal manure. To be of maximum benefit to your plants, manure should be applied only when it is well rotted. Liquid manure (made from a solution of manure in water) is another effective means of fertilizing your plants. A well-made compost should have all the elements essential for healthy growth. If a 2.5 cm (1 in) layer is added in spring and twice more during the growing season, it will not only provide sufficient nutrients to the plant but will also improve the consistency and drainage of the soil.

There is much to be said for organic and inorganic fertilizing, as both provide the nutrients that plants require. However, it may be best to try out both before making a final decision.

There is a distinct difference between potting on and repotting.

Potting on means that the plant has become too large for its present container and needs to be taken out and transferred to a larger pot.

Repotting means taking out the plant, pruning the rootball (and dividing it, if necessary), and replacing the soil in the same pot with a fresh mixture.

POTTING ON

While your plants are growing well you may justifiably sit back and enjoy their presence. But one day they may show symptoms of distress – leaves not quite as green and lush as they should be; a mass of roots making it difficult to water the soil; and, on turning the pot over, you may see roots creeping through the drainage holes. All these are signs that it is time for potting on.

Most plants do not like to be root bound, but they also do not like to be planted into a pot much larger than their existing one. A larger pot will retain more water and food than the roots can absorb and the soil will become sour and unhealthy. When potting on, the new pot should be one or at most two sizes larger.

To prepare the new pot for planting, place rocks and a layer of coarse sand in the bottom of the pot. This

POTTING ON MADE EASY

Step 1: Place drainage material plus a layer of potting soil in the base of the new pot.

Step 2: Without removing the plant from its old pot, place this pot onto the base layer. It should be placed in the centre, with its upper rim level with that of the new pot.

Step 3: Firmly pack the potting soil mix into the gap surrounding the old pot.

Step 4: Gently remove the old pot, leaving a hole which is the exact shape and size of the pot.

Step 5: Remove the plant from its old pot, trim the roots if necessary, then place it in the hole. It should fit perfectly.

Step 6: Top with a layer of soil and firm it lightly to anchor the plant.

will keep the drainage holes clear and excess water will be able to drain away. Add a layer of rotted leaves and then a layer of soil. If you want to use a pot liner (this keeps in the soil but lets through the water), make sure you place this inside the pot before adding the soil.

If you are still learning about house plant care it may be easier to follow the illustrated step-by-step procedure opposite.

If you are more *au fait* with caring for indoor plants, pot on as follows:

Water the plant before taking it out of its old pot. Trim back any weak or straggling roots and remove as much as possible of the old soil. Place the plant in the new pot and add soil, making sure that it reaches the same level as before. Firm the soil lightly around the plant to ensure the roots are in contact with the soil – do not tamp it down as this could damage the roots. Water well, and, a little later, check on the soil level (if it has dropped, add some more soil and water lightly). If the soil medium is of good quality you will only need to add fertilizer once the plant is well established.

REPOTTING

Some plants prefer smaller containers but once their roots have used up the nutrients in the soil they need to be repotted. This means taking the plant out of its pot and placing it in a new pot of the same size with a fresh soil mixture. If the plant is too large, the roots can be pruned to allow space for the potting mixture.

Hold the stem between your fingers, turn the pot upside down and gently tap the side and bottom of the pot to dislodge the plant. If you water the plant about half an hour before repotting, it will be easier to remove it from the pot.

Clear any green growth from the top of the soil and cut away any dead or damaged roots. If the rootball needs pruning to allow space for the new potting mixture, cut a thin slice off the bottom and each side of the rootball with a sharp knife.

Place a layer of rocks and coarse sand at the bottom of the pot and then add a layer of potting soil. Position the plant in the pot, add the remaining mixture and lightly firm the soil to anchor the plant. Water well.

Keep in mind that repotting will inhibit growth at first. Water the plants sparingly until they have re-established themselves and do not give extra food until strong, new leaves have appeared.

DIVIDING PLANTS

Just as pruning encourages new and vigorous growth, so too does the division of a pot-bound plant.

Remove the old plant from its pot and divide it into sections. Clumps can be divided by gently pulling the plants apart or, in the case of rhizomes such as *Aspidistras*, these can be cleanly cut through with a sharp knife or secateurs. Maidenhair ferns have masses of roots which can be cut into sections and replanted in individual pots. Bulbous plants can be separated and repotted – dust with a fungicide, place on a bed of sand, and cover.

A plant that has been left in the same pot for many years may have become weak. When dividing such plants, only the outer, healthier growth should be replanted.

Step 1: Hold the stem between your fingers, turn the pot over and gently remove the plant. Shake off any loose soil and remove stones or other drainage material which may have become entangled in the roots.

Step 2: Hold the rootball in both hands and slowly pull it apart. Make sure that all new sections have a portion of roots and stem.

Step 3: Place each section in its own pot and fill with soil. Firm the soil to anchor the plants, and water well.

Many people shy away from this procedure but it can be exciting and rewarding to produce new plants from old. It can also save a great deal of money. There are several ways to propagate plants.

GROWING PLANTS FROM SEED

Seeds can be grown in trays or in separate pots. These should be filled to within 2 cm (¾ in) of the top of the container with seedling mix or a mixture of two parts of sieved compost and one part of coarse, clean sand or vermiculite. Level the surface and sow the seeds in shallow furrows or sprinkle them over the surface. Cover with fine sand or soil and water well – this can be done either with a very fine spray or by placing the entire tray in shallow water so that the water can be drawn up into the soil.

The tray should then be covered with glass or newspaper. The newspaper should be removed as soon as germination has taken place, and the glass should be gradually raised after the first leaves have formed, then removed altogether when the seedlings have four leaves. It is essential to thin out the seedlings at this stage. Carefully lift the young plants and place them in other trays.

Water the plants lightly and regularly. Prevent damping off (caused by a fungus which grows at ground level and kills off young seedlings), by dusting or spraying the seedlings with a good fungicide.

Once the growth in the transplanted seedlings is strong, they can be given a weekly dose of watery liquid manure (the colour of weak tea). When they are a good size, they can be transferred into their permanent pots, which should be filled with a good potting mixture.

GROWING PLANTS FROM CUTTINGS

These can be taken from new growth (tip cuttings) or from mature growth (woody cuttings or leaf cuttings).

LEAF CUTTINGS

These cause great surprise to the uninitiated as it is hard to believe that an African violet leaf placed into soil can produce a group of new plants. *Begonias* and *Streptocarpus* can also be propagated successfully by leaf cuttings, and the leaves of succulents will grow easily if planted upright in damp, clean sand.

Ferns bear spores on the undersides of their leaves and when these are mature the entire leaf can be removed and laid on the surface of a tray that has been filled with a

African violets can be propagated simply by inserting the leaf stem in soil.

Step 1: To grow new plants from leaf cuttings cut the veins on the undersides of the leaves with a sharp blade.

Step 2: Lay the leaves, facing upwards, in a tray of damp sand, and secure them with small pieces of wire.

Step 3: Cover the tray with plastic to retain moisture, leaving it in place until new plants develop. Check every so often to make sure the soil remains damp.

rich and porous soil mixture. Water well and cover the entire tray with plastic or glass to keep the soil moist. Shield-like plants will soon cover the surface and from these new ferns will arise. When sufficiently grown, the young plants can be transferred carefully into their own trays or pots.

TIP CUTTINGS

As the name suggests, these are taken from the tips of stems where there is tender new growth. Cuttings should be about 10 cm (4 in) in length. Remove the lower leaves and plant the cuttings in clean, coarse sand. If preferred, they can be dipped into hormone powder first (available from nurseries and garden centres). Keep them damp but not waterlogged, and transplant them into their own pots when they have developed a good root system.

Plants that can be grown by means of tip cuttings include *Aphelandra* (page 59), *Browallia* (page 65), *Codiaeum* (page 71), *Fatsia* (page 80), *Hedera* (page 83), *Impatiens* (page 85), *Plectranthus* (page 94) and *Schefflera* (page 99).

WOODY CUTTINGS

Woody cuttings are taken from mature stems and the cuttings should be a bit (about 15–20 cm/6–8 in) longer than tip cuttings.

This form of propagation can also be used with the aforementioned plants.

Chlorophytum comosum (page 69) sends out long stems which develop new plantlets at the ends. These new plants can be planted into small pots and, when new growth develops (a sign of the plant being established), the connecting stem can be cleanly cut through.

A **colourful display of** bulbs that flower in late winter or early spring can brighten up any home at a time when there is usually very little colour around. Bulbs can be grown in containers or pots but the secret to success is to ensure that they are kept cool (the temperature should not exceed 6–8 °C/ 43–46 °F) and dark for 6–10 weeks after planting.

Winter and spring bulbs, corms and tubers are often on sale from summer but they should not be planted until early autumn when the weather is cooler. Treated bulbs should be planted in late autumn. It is best to buy bulbs that are recommended for indoor cultivation and to check them to make sure that they are a good size, firm and free of any signs of disease.

The soil should be friable, have good drainage, and should have superphosphate and bone meal added to it for extra nourishment. Put a layer of moist compost in the bottom of the container and place the bulbs on top of this. The bulbs should be placed close to one another but should not touch each other or the sides of the container. Add the soil mixture, firming it lightly around the bulbs, until the soil level is about 1 cm (½ in) from the rim of the pot. The bulbs should be planted to twice their depth. Cover the pot with a black plastic bag and place it in a cool, dark place, checking occasionally to make sure that the soil is still damp. After approximately 6–10 weeks the container can be brought indoors and placed in a shady spot at first and then moved to a brighter (not sunny) position. The leaves will begin to develop and after a few weeks the buds should appear.

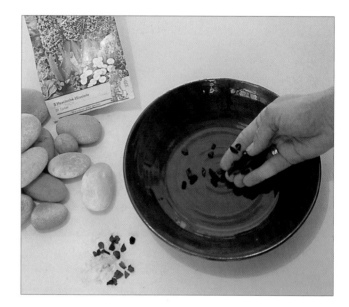

Step 1: Place a thin layer of soil and compost in the base of a shallow bowl. Charcoal pieces should be added to absorb any excess minerals and ensure a healthy, balanced soil mix.

Step 2: Arrange clean river pebbles on top of the soil layer, making sure that they fill the entire bowl.

Step 3: Place the hyacinth bulbs on the pebbles. The bulbs should be placed in an upright position and should not touch one another or the edge of the bowl.

Step 4: Fill the bowl with water so that it covers the pebbles and is in contact with the base of the bulbs. Place the bowl in a dark, cool place until the first leaves appear. Move the bowl to its chosen position and keep the water level constant.

These plants should be watered regularly and extra liquid manure should be applied when the first leaves are growing well.

Bulbs such as liliums, freesias or ixias can either be planted on their own, or they can be mixed with other bulbs or annuals. However, make sure that their flowering times coincide. When planting annuals, for example lobelias, Virginia stocks, pansies or violas, bring the plants into strong light indoors once the leaves of the bulbs have appeared. When mixing bulbs, place daffodil bulbs, for example, in the base – one or two layers should be sufficient – then plant lower-growing bulbs such as Muscari or Lachenalia in the upper layer.

Hyacinth bulbs can be planted on pebbles or gravel (see step-by-step method), in soil and in water. If planting in soil, make sure that the mix is rich and fertile and has good drainage. Half of the bulb should show above the soil's surface. Special hyacinth jars, available at nurseries and garden centres, hold the bulb in place so that it just touches the water surface. Store the bulbs in a cool, dark place until the first leaves appear. From this time it is essential to keep the water level constant.

acti and succulents are ideal plants for indoor cultivation as they require little care and can be used with striking decorative effect.

Their natural habitat is the desert or semi-desert where the soil is sandy and the sun extremely hot for most of the year. They have adapted to these adverse conditions by producing fleshy stems and leaves for storing water, and in some cases thorns have replaced the leaves to prevent loss of moisture from the plant.

They should be placed in a sunny position near a window but need to be moved in winter as they could be damaged by the cold.

The soil must have excellent drainage as any water that collects around the roots will soon rot them. Coarse sand and compost is a good mix. Although these plants come from areas where water is scarce, they should be given a thorough drenching every two to three weeks.

An arrangement of cacti or succulents looks its best when the plants are mixed according to size variation and are grown in containers of pebbles or stones. Cacti and succulents usually flower in winter or early spring. There are also several species, such as *Kalanchoe blossfeldiana* and *K.* 'Tessa', which make a beautiful display of their trailing stems when planted in hanging baskets.

HOW TO PLANT A CACTUS

Step 1: Place a layer of small stones in the base of the pot to ensure good drainage.

Step 2: Fill the pot with soil (the soil mix should be made up of potting soil and coarse river sand), and plant the cactus. If the cactus has sharp spines, wrap newspaper around it to protect your hands.

Step 3: Place white river stones on the surface to keep the soil in place and to create a stark decorative contrast.

Potted cacti can be displayed creatively on a sunny wall. Simply fasten the pots to the wall with brackets.

Many house plants need pruning or cutting back to maintain a neat and attractive appearance. There are different ways of maintaining a plant's shape and it is important to use the correct method to ensure that your plants remain compact yet healthy.

PINCHING OUT

This method entails pinching out the growing tips of the plant and is usually used on long-stemmed plants or climbers to create a more compact or bushy appearance. As a new terminal bud appears, gently nip it out with your fingers. This will encourage side growth.

PRUNING AND CUTTING BACK

These methods are used to cut back any excessive or unwanted growth and are best done in spring. This can be very beneficial to the plants as any weak, dead or diseased growth can be cut back completely to allow room for healthy, new growth. Always use a sharp pair of scissors or secateurs and remember to cut just above a growth bud.

DEAD-HEADING

As soon as a flower has wilted or faded it should be removed from the plant. This will encourage new blooms and maintain a neat appearance.

Plants should be neat and compact to maintain an attractive display – dead or damaged leaves should be removed, straggling growth should be cut back, and leaves should be cleaned regularly with a damp cloth.

Support is usually obtained from the soil, through which the roots grow to form an anchor for the plant. Supports are essential for climbing plants, but there are also certain tall-growing plants with brittle stems that may snap or bend if they are not given extra support.

To support a tall plant, drive a stake deep into the soil to anchor it and tie the plant to the stake with raffia or string. The string should be tied loosely around the stem, then around the support in a figure of eight. The stem should never be placed up against the support and tied with just one loop as this could result in restriction or damage to the stem.

A climbing plant will eventually grow beyond the confines of its pot and will need to be given some direction and support. Once again, the support must be placed deep in the pot for good anchorage. Supports for climbers include sticks, frames of wood or plastic, and moss sticks (made by enclosing moss in a cylinder of wire, see page 32). For the more vigorous climbers, a trellis may be necessary. A climber framing a window can look lovely but the plant will need to be given direction by means of wires or wooden supports. The new growth should be trained to grow around the support before it becomes too long and difficult to bend.

Climbers and tall plants with brittle stems require some kind of support, such as the trellis and moss stick featured here.

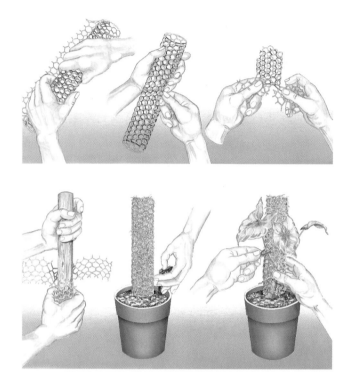

Moss sticks provide support for larger climbing plants.

Step 1: Roll a rectangular section of chicken wire into a tubular shape.

Step 2: Fasten the loose edge of the chicken wire by folding the jutting pieces into the centre of the tube.

Step 3: Cut one end of the tube and bend back the wire. Cover the other end.

Step 4: Fill the inside of the tube with sphagnum moss or coir (coconut) fibre (available from nurseries and garden centres), and push it down with a stick to firm it.

Step 5: Close the tube and stand it in the centre of a pot, wedging it in place with soil.

Step 6: Place the plant in position and fasten the long stems to the moss stick with pieces of bent wire.

PESTS AND DISEASES

Because house plants are kept in confined spaces, they will be attacked by pests and diseases from time to time. If you check your plants regularly you will be able to detect most pests and diseases in their early stages and they can be dealt with before causing serious damage.

Chemical pesticides and fungicides are most commonly used in eradicating insect pests and fungal diseases. However, there are also a number of environmentally friendly, non-chemical products that are equally effective, and it is worthwhile making enquiries at your local nursery or garden centre to find out what is available.

FUNGAL DISEASES
Fungal diseases are caused by insufficient air circulation and can spread at an alarming rate if not dealt with immediately. Botrytis (grey mould) thrives where there is poor air circulation and can cover the plant with unsightly and destructive mould. As soon as any signs of grey mould are detected, remove and destroy the affected parts and spray the plant with fungicide.

POWDERY MILDEW
Powdery mildew appears as a white or grey powder on the upper surface of the leaves but may also be found on flowers and stems. It is usually caused by a sudden drop in temperature, poor ventilation and high humidity. Once the mildew has taken hold it can distort new growth and cause leaves to dry out. Remove every affected part of the plant and destroy it. Apply a good

fungicide, not only to the plant, but to the soil as well. Do this every ten days until every trace of the disease has disappeared.

PESTS

SCALE

Scale insects have hard, yellow-brown shells and are found on stems and leaf stalks where they suck out the sap. They do not need specific conditions in which to thrive and can be difficult to eradicate if left untreated so it is best to check regularly for signs of infestation. If caught in the early stages, scale can be effectively treated with a solution of half methylated spirits and half water. Saturate cotton wool or a paint brush with the solution and apply it over the affected area. This will loosen the scale, which can then be scraped off with a stick. When all the scale has been removed, treat the plant with insecticide.

MEALY BUGS

Mealy bugs have a soft, white covering of downy fluff and are usually found where the leaf stalk joins the stem. They suck sap from the plants and a prolonged infestation can cause leaves to yellow, wilt and fall. They thrive in warm, moist conditions. A spray of soapy water or the application of a solution of half methylated spirits and half water can be effective if the pests are dealt with at an early stage. However, if the infestation has spread to most of the plant it is best to treat it with insecticide.

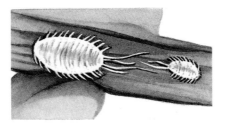

APHIDS

These insects are soft, green and fat, and may or may not have wings. They suck the sap from tender new shoots, which leads to distorted growth, and may also transmit diseases from one plant to another. At the first sign, rub them off with your fingers, but if they have been allowed to become too great in number, spray lightly with soapy water or, if absolutely essential, use an insecticide.

WHITEFLY

These insect pests are difficult to treat as they lurk on the undersides of leaves. They suck sap from the leaves and excrete a sticky residue, which can lead to the growth of sooty mould. The adults and nymphs can be successfully treated with a spray of insecticide but the larvae are unaffected by this method. The only way to eradicate them entirely is to wait for the larvae to mature and spray the plant every ten days until there is no further sign of infestation.

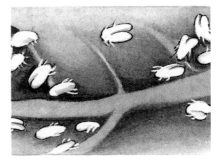

RED SPIDER MITES

These tiny insects are barely visible to the naked eye but they can be detected by the webs they create on the undersides of leaves. They thrive in dry conditions so a humid atmosphere and regular mist-spraying will usually keep them at bay. Treat an infested plant with regular sprays of water over a period of about two weeks. Only use an insecticide if the infestation is severe.

DECORATING
WITH HOUSE PLANTS

Plants will fit into any decor, be it modern or traditional. There is not a room in the house that cannot be enhanced by the addition of plants, but it is necessary to make a commitment to look after them. There is nothing that detracts more from a room than a half-dead plant in a boring pot.

Including plants as part of your interior design can make all the difference and emphasize the style you wish to create. Hanging baskets of ferns can be placed in a bay window to create a Victorian style, and a solitary *Ficus benjamina* or palm in a terracotta or ceramic pot can be strategically positioned on a tiled floor to create an elegant and opulent look to the modern home.

The selection of plants is important and if you are in any doubt about what to choose advice can always be obtained from nurseries or garden centres as to which plants are best suited to the growing conditions in your home.

Containers add the finishing touch to any display of indoor plants and it is worthwhile taking your time when making a selection from the enormous variety available.

If you visit a specialist house-plant nursery you will discover a large number of plants, all of which have been grown specifically for indoor cultivation. Without a clear idea of what you want or need it can be difficult to make a choice.

Choosing plants for your home can be frustrating, but it can also be exciting. What you need to do is take your time and think about every aspect of the plant – its height, spread and colour (there are many shades of green), as well as its need for light, warmth and humidity.

Most flowering plants need to be positioned in bright light or direct sun.

If you are growing house plants for the first time it is a good idea to keep a look out for the words 'easy to grow'. Once you have grown a few of these you will be hooked on house plants and will enjoy meeting the challenges offered by those species that have a reputation of being more difficult to grow.

LIGHT

Light is one of the most important factors to consider when choosing a plant for it is useless placing a plant that needs sun in a dark corner. However, if you want a sun-loving plant in a particular dark corner, there is a solution to the problem. Growing lights (see page 13) not only give the plant the necessary amount of light for growth, but can make the corner, together with its plant, a focal point. An *Alocasia* has huge leaves and if it is placed in a suitable pot and is lit up at night it can look spectacular.

SPACE

The space available will influence which plants you can use – would a slender palm be suitable, or is there room for a spreading *Ficus*? Plants are an asset in any home but they can be a nuisance if they become overgrown. It is therefore important to find out how large they will grow.

A plant with tall, slender growth can be placed where space is limited.

SHAPE

The shape of the growth should also be considered. A *Dieffenbachia*, with its uncompromising erect growth and large leaves, differs greatly in appearance from a trailing

This orchid with its stark silhouette would be suitable in a modern, minimalist interior.

fine, feathery leaves create a soft look, while plants with gigantic leaves create a dramatic appearance. You can also highlight a delicate climbing plant by grouping it with another with large leaves.

LEAF SHAPE

There are long strap-like leaves, perfectly round leaves, spiky palm leaves, delicate maidenhair fern leaves and gigantic fig leaves. Leaf shape has a strong influence on the effectiveness of an arrangement of plants and can be used to create the focal point of the display. Interesting decorative effects can be brought about by combining contrasting shapes or by using shapes that complement one another.

ivy or a shimmering maidenhair fern. Some house plants resemble small trees and have a central stem and side branches – these usually look their best when placed on their own. Other plants are dense, bushy and round, or have their leaves close to the ground. These plants can be grouped around taller plants to create an interesting effect. Decide which shape would best suit the space you have available before you buy any new plants.

LEAF COLOUR

The colours of leaves are many and varied. While you may say that all leaves are green, you only need to look at a group of plants to see the

LEAVES

There are so many things to consider and so many plants to choose from, but leaves will probably have the greatest effect on your choice of plants. Shape, size and colour are the most important factors when decorating with leaves. With the myriad leaf and plant shapes available you can make a statement by using a single plant, or by bringing different plants together. Whatever you choose to do, you can use your house plants to create an atmosphere to suit your lifestyle, as well as provide an easy and inexpensive way of decorating your home.

LEAF SIZE

What about the size of the leaves? Some may be no larger than a small coin while others can be huge. Some of the best decorative effects can be created by grouping plants with a similar leaf size together, but emphasizing the size difference can be equally effective. Ferns with

The colour, shape and size of the leaves are important factors to consider when choosing a new plant.

many different shades. By grouping different species with contrasting leaf colours you can create various decorative effects and add interest to an otherwise ordinary room.

Variegated leaves of gold and green, silver and green, pink and green, and many other colour combinations, can be used to make a pleasing display of foliage plants. However, take care not to bring too many of them into one grouping as this could cause a distressing muddle of colour. It is better to use just one or two variegated plants in a combination with single-colour plants. Lightly coloured, variegated plants such as the golden *Nephrolepis* fern or golden variegated *Schefflera* can be used on their own to brighten up a dull corner of the room.

Grey leaves are a delight to gardeners who use them to soften bright colours or to act as a link between different colours. For example, if you place a grey-leaved *Aglaonema* with a dark-leaved *Spathiphyllum* you will be able to create a lighter and softer effect.

LEAF TEXTURE

Leaf texture can also be used within a display. The leaf texture can be matte or shiny, hairy or smooth, ribbed or wrinkled. Glossy leaves throw back the light and give a much more lively effect than matte leaves or leaves that

When selecting plants, choose species with unusual leaf texture and coloration like this variegated *Aglaonema*.

are covered with fine hairs. A grouping of plants with matte leaves produces a soothing and tranquil atmosphere, but just one plant with shining leaves placed among them will immediately add a dramatic effect.

FLOWERING PLANTS

Flowering plants add colour to your home and should be considered when selecting plants. However, the size, shape and colour of the flowers, as well as their flowering time, will influence your selection. Most flowering plants bloom in spring or summer, but there are a few that flower all year round. However, it is worthwhile considering those species that flower in winter as their colour can be a pleasure at a time when there is very little of it around. Ask for advice at your local nursery or garden centre as to which flowering plants are best suited to your needs.

Flowering plants like this pretty pelargonium should be positioned in a sunny spot to prolong their blooming period.

BUYING PLANTS

aving decided which plants to buy and where they are going to be placed, it is wise to make a list of what you want before going to the garden centre. Once there, you should be very selective for the plants you want should look immediately attractive. Below is a list of things to remember and to look out for when buying new plants.

- Buy plants from a reputable nursery that stocks healthy plants.
- Look for plants with healthy green leaves that are free of any signs of pests or diseases.
- Flowering plants should have healthy, fat buds, not shrivelled ones.

- Look at the underside of the pot to make sure that the roots are not creeping through.
- Shrubs should have a good overall growth. Those with old, woody stems will detract from the appearance.
- Give plants a gentle tug to ensure that the roots are established and the plant has not been newly potted.
- Look out for algae or moss on the soil's surface as this is a sure sign of neglect.
- Take new plants home as soon as possible. Do not keep them in a very hot or very cold car for too long.
- Transport plants in individual plastic bags to protect the foliage and minimize mess.
- Once the plants have been placed in their new home look after them as best you can.

Modern nurseries and garden centres have a large variety of plants suitable for indoors, and knowledge-able staff to help you select the right plants for your home.

House plant containers are legion and, although they may at first appear to be expensive, they are a worthwhile investment as a permanent asset in the home and as an inherent part of the decor.

Many materials and substances have been brought into use in the making of plant containers and pots. Apart from those available in shops, householders delight in finding something different and unusual for holding their plants. Old preserving pans and kettles of copper or brass, cast-iron pots and ceramic dishes are just some of the articles that can be used to make interesting containers.

TERRACOTTA

Terracotta pots have been used for centuries for storing food and oil, and are still highly regarded for their classic lines. Foliage and flowering plants look stunning in terracotta, and a group of containers of different shapes and heights will create great interest and visual pleasure. Terracotta can be used to provide a contrast with modern furnishings, or to blend subtly with cottage furniture.

Terracotta is often used in the classic urn shape: tall, with rounded shoulders narrowing to the base. This style is suitable for a tall slender shrub which is approximately one and a half times the height of the container. Low-growing plants can be planted around the base of the shrub.

A word of warning: The mouth of this urn is much narrower than the base and when the time comes to remove the tree or shrub, it could cause a problem. Slow-growing plants that do not need to be potted on for a few years are best suited to this type of container.

Even these rusty old enamel bowls look charming when planted with bright flowers.

White lilies (*Lilium longiflorum*) look elegant and lovely in a tall terracotta pot. Being seasonal and needing strong light, they are best planted in a separate bag or pot, then placed in the urn when they are about to flower. They will make a striking contrast with poinsettias (*Euphorbia pulcherrima*), which have been induced to flower at Christmas time. Ivy can be encouraged to cascade down all sides of an urn, as can *Asparagus densiflorus* spp.

Rounded terracotta pots are suited to many types of plants. *Chlorophyton* with its pendant stems, or a small *Ficus benjamina* with plaited stems, looks especially good in this style container. Colourful *Pelargoniums* also look wonderful in these natural, earthy pots. Try grouping the tall and slender containers with the wide and shallow ones and include a tray of water and pebbles to add interest (this will also help keep up humidity levels). Even the old-fashioned pots with the sloping sides look charming when planted with herbs or simple flowers.

FIBRE CEMENT

These containers are available in a wide range of styles and often have complex mouldings. They are light and easy to move but can be damaged by careless handling. Fibre cement is not very durable and constant dampness can cause damage, but if the pots are looked after they can last for many years. Containers with slender necks and flared bases need particularly careful handling as they can snap off at the neck.

Fibre cement has a natural grey colour which is similar to stone or concrete, but it can be painted or decorated in whatever style or colour you choose. The advantage of

There is a wide selection of containers available at nurseries and garden centres and you should consider the effect you wish to achieve before deciding on which container best suits your plant.

this is that the paint can be changed whenever you choose – at Christmas time, for example, the glistening white pot that holds your Christmas tree can be sprinkled with gold or silver.

CONCRETE

Concrete is not only used in the building industry and should not be considered dull and lifeless. It has been used to fashion many elegant containers with finely moulded decorations resembling carved stone. Apart from plant containers and pots, concrete has been used to make statues and other house or garden ornaments, some of which hold bowls for planting. As these are extremely heavy, they must be carefully placed – do not position them on a carpet as they will leave permanent impressions.

The range of basketware is extensive. Baskets can be lined and planted with a mix of flowering and foliage plants, or filled with small pots of herbs or roses.

PLASTIC

Plastic pots are often regarded as unacceptable for house plants, but this substance has been used to produce attractive and colourful containers, some with decorative mouldings. A matte look is also available, and is more appealing than the older glossy pots.

A plastic pot is easier to handle than a black plastic bag and can be used as a 'holder' for a plant before placing it in another container. It can then be taken out at will whenever you need to tidy the plant. Plastic containers retain water better than most other materials and plants therefore need less frequent waterings.

CERAMIC

Ceramic containers have a definite place in the home and there is such a wonderful selection from which to choose.

Fibre cement pots are found in all shapes and sizes and can be painted to suit your decor.

Eastern designs, but there are many others which will enhance the look of these splendid pots.

When grouping glazed ceramic pots it is wise not to overdo it. Keep to one or two colours, with perhaps just one highly decorated pot as a focal point. Sometimes it looks good to have just one Eastern jar or pot on its own to make a statement in its corner, or to match the carpet or curtains.

Old Victorian jardinières, many of them with their own ornate stands, are coming back into fashion. They can be bought at second-hand stores or on auction sales. An *Aspidistra* with full and luxuriant foliage will look beautiful planted in one of these. A potted *Begonia* planted in a rose-covered dish will be a fine addition to the bathroom decor, as will a trailing plant in an old tureen placed on top of the shower wall. One or two *Streptocarpus* in full flower placed in an old jardinière will make a pretty centrepiece for the dining table.

BASKETWARE

These containers are well suited to the cottage look. The delicate tracery of a finely woven shallow basket will be a fine foil for a group of African violets or primulas, or for a mixture of flowering and foliage plants. Sturdy baskets of cane or woven vines will show off brightly coloured *Pelargoniums* or a variegated, small-leafed ivy. Larger baskets of woven grass or palm leaves, as well as those tall lugs that were used for carrying grapes, can be used as outer containers for tall plants such as palms. They look outstanding when placed on a covered patio or in a large kitchen.

Large baskets can be lined with watertight plastic sheeting, buckets or containers. Smaller baskets can be lined with foil.

Giant-sized baskets, with or without handles, can be planted with groupings of plants of varying heights and leaf textures.

A basket lined with decorative paper and filled with an assortment of plants will make a wonderful gift and, if small pots of sweet-smelling herbs are included, it will be all the more welcome.

A low, oval basket filled with small pots of scented *Pelargoniums*, mint and thyme, placed between vases filled with sweet-smelling roses, will create a delightful centrepiece for the lunch or breakfast table. A painted

From the East has come a fine assemblage of ceramic containers, many of them decorated with ornate and intricate designs. These are quite expensive but most of them can be regarded as works of art due to the high standard of workmanship and quality finishes. This also applies to the work of local ceramicists, whose products are on display in many nurseries and garden centres. Many have flower motifs, but there are also those that are more plainly decorated, and thus suitable for a larger selection of plants.

When using pots that are highly decorated it is advisable to use only foliage plants to avoid a fussy look. Palm trees and bamboo seem to complement basket with pots of African violets or those endearing miniature roses that come in tiny plastic pots is a wonderful addition to any room.

HANGING BASKETS

These are useful where space is limited. Heavy baskets should have a strong support in the way of a hook in the ceiling and wire or rope from which to suspend the basket. A fisherman's swivel inserted between the end of the rope and the basket will allow the basket to turn without twisting the rope or wire.

Although it is common practice to place plastic in the base of the basket to prevent dripping, it is better to take down baskets before watering.

Metal hanging baskets containing plastic bowls for planting are useful as they do not drip water onto the floor. Spend some time looking around to see what is available and which style will best suit your home.

GALVANIZED IRON

This metal has been fashioned into buckets and baths by local craftsmen and is much in demand. The containers can be placed on the floor or suspended as hanging baskets. If you wish to paint them, they must first be treated with galvanized iron pre-cleaner (available from hardware stores), which will remove the galvanizing and allow paint to adhere to the surface. These unusual containers can be decorated with flowers or other designs, lending an air of informality to the kitchen or bathroom.

Enamelled pot holders planted with trailing foliage plants will look wonderful if placed on kitchen shelves.

WOOD

Wood can be used to make planters but these will need inner containers to prevent rotting. Left unpainted, wood has a look of permanence and is equally fitting for formal or informal furnishings.

Old or modern wine barrels take up a lot of space but lend an old-world atmosphere to old homes that have been restored to their former glory. They look superb on an enclosed patio when planted with *Hydrangeas* or *Camellias* and, where the kitchen is vast, a wine barrel planted with a giant *Spathiphyllum* is gracious and lovely. Old fern or palm stands made of oak or teak add that extra slender height which is so useful in small rooms.

Unlike terracotta or concrete, plastic is not absorbent, thus plants need to be watered less frequently.

GLASS

Glass containers are unusual but interesting receptacles for house plants. Ferns or other green foliage plants can be planted in a layer of fertile soil in the base of an all-glass fish-tank, which will soon take on an all-green appearance. A hyacinth bulb placed on top of a tall glass container will send its roots down into the water to create a fascinating pattern (see page 46).

BRASS AND COPPER

These pots are perfect as outer containers and create a beautiful contrast when planted with ferns and other green trailing plants.

MATCHING PLANTS TO CONTAINERS

 he shape and style of the container should suit the plant that will be placed in it. It is also important to match the plant and container to the setting: a fern planted in a classic urn will not suit a modern interior, whereas a low terracotta dish planted with a ponytail palm will match the fashionable setting.

Container shapes range from tall and slender to low and wide, and a sense of proportion in relation to the plant's growth should be kept in mind. The normal scale is for the plant to be one and a half times the height or width of the container. For example, a low, creeping plant is better suited to a wide, shallow bowl than a tall pot.

Sometimes a plant is obtained before a container, in which case it is a good idea to spend some time looking at the various options. You can even take your plant along to the garden centre – the staff will gladly advise you as to which container would best suit your plant.

Below left: Orchids in aluminium pots create a stark, modern effect. Ensure the soil has good drainage as these plants require frequent watering.
Below: Hyacinth bulbs grown in glass containers (see page 27).
Opposite: Interesting effects can be created by matching the plant to its container and the setting.

Herbs can be grown in almost any container in a sunny kitchen or bathroom if they are regularly tended and watered. They are not only functional in that they can be used for cooking or medicinal purposes but, if chosen correctly, can fill the room with a subtle, aromatic blend of fragrances.

When creating a herb planter you should be guided by which herbs suit your needs. If you want a planter for culinary use, consider herbs such as basil, rosemary and origanum. A medicinal planter, for example, could include comfrey, lavender and mint, and a fragrant planter marjoram, pineapple sage and thyme.

Even if you don't have space for a small herb garden, an arrangement of potted culinary herbs can be grown in any kitchen providing there is sufficient light. The advantage of this is that they are readily available when you are cooking and, in addition to being functional, make a beautiful living feature.

Herbs are also used for medicinal and therapeutic purposes and can be brewed into teas, applied in hot or cold compresses and steeped into steam inhalers as alternatives or supports to conventional therapies. Create a medicine chest with a difference using therapeutic herbs – comfrey and lemon thyme – and aromatic herbs – rejuvenating mint, and lavender, which treats a variety of complaints including restlessness, insomnia and a broken heart!

Below and below left: An old medicine cabinet or antique biscuit tin can be used to display culinary or medicinal herbs.
Opposite: Crates, cigar boxes and terracotta pots make up this kitchen herb garden of sweet basil, pineapple sage and apple mint for salads; marjoram, origanum and penny royal for soups and stews; and traditional parsley and garlic chives.

FRIDGE MAGNETS

This 'fridge garden' can be planted using cuttings from almost any house plant. These temporary miniatures are a fun alternative to more traditional house plants and are useful where space is limited (do not use glass containers if you have small children). The cuttings need little water and can be kept in their holders for up to eight weeks before they need to be replaced (you can discard them or replant them in permanent pots) – this allows you to change the display at will.

Step 1: You need a selection of small, light containers that can be transformed into fridge magnets by glueing a piece of magnetic strip to the back.

Step 2: Cuttings can be planted in a mixture of potting soil and small drainage stones, or can be grown in water.

Step 3: Arrange the miniatures on your fridge either as novelty magnets or as a fantasy garden (opposite).

PLANTING AN INDOOR WINDOW BOX

Indoor **window boxes** are an effective way of brightening up a plain window or, in fact, any area of your home. For year-round colour choose flowering perennials such as African violets and combine them with other foliage plants that require the same growing conditions.

Step 1: To prepare the window box for planting, place river stones in the base of the container to ensure good drainage, and top this with a layer of potting soil. The window box should have a drip tray to prevent leakage.

Step 2: Place your plants in position while they are still in their pots and pack soil firmly around the containers.

Gently remove the pots: this will leave an even potting space in which to place the plant without disrupting or damaging the roots. Take the plants out of their pots and place them in the soil.

Step 3: Intersperse the African violets with pretty foliage plants ('Peace in the Home' has been used in this example). These fill the gaps between the African violets and contrast and complement the colour and texture of the plants.

Step 4: The window box is now ready to display. Make sure that the soil is kept damp and regularly trim off any dead leaves or flowers.

PLANTING A MIXED BASKET

A **mixed basket is** used to display a variety of flowering and foliage plants when they are at their best. It is important to group plants with colours and leaf textures which complement one another and which have similar growing conditions.

Step 1: You need a basket, a thick sheet of plastic, small drainage stones, a soil mix which is rich in compost, and a selection of flowering and foliage plants.

Step 2: Line the basket with thick plastic sheeting and trim it to size: allow a small overhang which can be tucked in at the end. Place drainage stones in the base and fill with soil.

Step 3: Arrange the plants before planting to make sure you are happy with the display. Once decided, ease the plants out of their pots, making sure not to damage the roots.

Step 4: Place the plants in position and lightly firm the soil around them to anchor the roots.

Step 5: When all the plants have been placed, tuck in the plastic sheeting and decorate the edge of the basket with sphagnum moss or coir (coconut) fibre. Take care not to over-water as there is no drainage.

DIRECTORY
OF HOUSE PLANTS

T he choice of plants to be included in this directory has been a difficult one in view of the large and ever-increasing selection of plants available for indoor cultivation.

Another difficult aspect to consider is that vastly different conditions exist in different households. One house may face south and another north, which greatly influences the amount of light available throughout the day. Also, even when the temperature inside different homes may be the same, the humidity levels can vary considerably.

The main objective, however, has been to arouse an enthusiasm for this fascinating occupation – that of bringing the garden indoors. As there are so many plants from which to choose, it is best to page through the entire directory and make a list of the plants that appeal to you. Go back to each of these entries and read up on these plants' requirements, then narrow down the list to the plants that match the growing conditions in your home. Some plants are easier to grow than others – *Aspidistras* and some ferns can tolerate a certain amount of neglect, whereas African violets need constant attention – and it is worth considering the easier option if this is the first time you will be bringing plants into your home.

Achimenes hybrids
Hot water plant

Adiantum raddianum
Delta maidenhair fern

This plant acquired its unusual common name because some growers plunge the entire container into hot (not boiling) water at the beginning of spring to encourage new growth. *Achimenes* have slender leafy stems bearing flowers at their tips. The flowers, with long tubes and velvety petals, bloom in midsummer and come in rich and vibrant colours, as well as pale pink and white. They are ideal for hanging baskets but also look impressive in ordinary containers.

Light This plant should be placed in an area with strong light and will even tolerate a little morning sun. There should be a free flow of air but no draughts.

Soil and water A soil mix with good drainage and regular watering during the growing season (spring to autumn) will ensure that the plant thrives. An application of weak liquid manure (the colour of weak tea) once every ten days in late spring will encourage healthy growth.

Temperature and humidity *Achimenes* like warm, humid growing conditions. Once growth is healthy and vigorous, they should not be allowed to dry out.

General care When flowering is over, let the plants die down gradually. Once they have completely dried out you will see that the tubers have multiplied. These can be stored in a dry, cool place until spring. At this stage, they can be planted in separate containers or baskets.

Pests and diseases Seldom attacked.

This fern has slender black stems and delicate, triangular green fronds, which shiver in the slightest breeze. The leaflets are pale pink when young and develop to a pale then dark green. When the plant matures, clusters of brown sporangia (spore sacs) appear on the undersides of the leaves. This fern can be used to soften a display or can be placed on its own.

Light A shady spot, away from direct sunlight, is best.

Soil and water A soil mixture with good drainage is essential. The fern should be kept moist at all times during spring and summer and into early autumn, but can be allowed a winter rest with minimal watering. Monthly applications of pot plant food during the growing season (late spring to autumn) should see to its needs, or you can administer a weak liquid manure every two weeks.

Temperature and humidity Maidenhair ferns can tolerate cold but there should be no sudden drop in temperature during the growing season. These plants thrive in humid conditions and a fine mist-spray of the surrounding air and the placing of a dish of water near to the plants, will raise the humidity during dry weather.

General care Dead fronds should be cut back regularly. These plants should not be allowed to become pot-bound and should be potted on in spring (see pages 22–23).

Pests and diseases Scale, mealy bugs and red spider mites (see page 33).

Aechmea fasciata
Urn plant

Aeschynanthus lobbianus
Lipstick plant

This is a member of the bromeliad family whose natural habitat is in the steamy forests of South America. These plants have wide, soft grey leaves powdered with silver, which come together to form a 'tank'. This 'tank' should be filled with water at all times. The pink flowers appear in late spring and can last for many weeks.

Light The light should be strong but there should be little or no direct sunlight. These plants also grow in semi-shade.

Soil and water The potting soil should be mixed with a generous portion of pine-bark chips, charcoal, vermiculite, or gravel to ensure good drainage. Although the plant likes moisture in the air and soil it does not tolerate soggy conditions. Liquid manure should be given once a week in the growing season (spring to autumn) but as winter approaches water and food should be cut down. New growth can be encouraged in spring by means of light watering for two or three weeks, and then plenty of water until autumn.

Temperature and humidity These warm-climate plants will not tolerate extreme cold and need to be protected in winter. Humidity should be high from spring to autumn.

General care Although *Aechmeas* are among the toughest and most tolerant of the bromeliads, they will produce healthier and more vigorous growth if given extra warmth and humidity.

Pests and diseases Scale (see page 33).

This species, with its striking tubular flowers and slightly fleshy leaves, is a member of a family of epiphytic plants from South-East Asia. It will cascade from a basket or can be trained to grow up a small frame or a moss stick.

Light This plant should be placed where the light is fairly strong, but not in direct sunlight.

Soil and water The soil mix should be loose and friable and have good drainage. Water regularly and feed with weak liquid manure from spring through to autumn.

Temperature and humidity Originating in a tropical climate, this plant does not tolerate low temperatures and should be protected during winter. It needs high humidity in both the air and the soil for most of the year but during winter the humidity should be reduced and the foliage kept dry to prevent fungal infections.

General care Dead flowers should be removed as they fade and stems can be cut back in spring or autumn to promote healthy regrowth.

Pests and diseases Aphids (see page 33).

Aglaonema 'Silver King'
No common name

Alocasia micholitziana
Elephant's ear

The name *aglaos* – bright, and *nema* – filament, refers to the shining stamens. These are handsome house plants with generous rosettes of grey-green leaves, which are patterned with white. *Aglaonemas* are adaptable plants that do well in air-conditioned homes or offices, provided they are given sufficient moisture in the air and in the soil. Another popular variety is *A. crispum.*

Light The leaves should not be exposed to direct sunlight as they prefer partial shade. The plant will even grow in a dark corner for a limited time.

Soil and water The rich soil mix should be damp at all times, but never waterlogged, and should have good drainage. During winter, however, the plant should only be given an occasional watering and should be allowed to go into partial dormancy. A feed of pot plant food every six weeks during the growing season (spring to early autumn) should be sufficient.

Temperature and humidity As these plants come from the tropical climate of East Asia, *Aglaonemas* need warmth and humidity, and a sudden drop in temperature could cause leaf tips and edges to turn brown. Spray the leaves or wipe them with a clean wet cloth to keep them damp.

General care Clumps can be divided and repotted in spring (see page 23).

Pests and diseases Mealy bugs (see page 33).

In a spacious setting it makes an outstanding feature plant with its long fleshy stems and large dark-green leaves, which are heavily veined in white. Care should be taken to place the plant where its leaves cannot be damaged by passers-by or draughts. Other popular but larger species include *A. gigantea* and *A. macrorrhiza.*

Light This plant needs strong to medium light, with no direct sunlight except in the morning.

Soil and water The soil should be enriched with compost and have good drainage. Plenty of water during the growing season (spring to autumn) is essential. Regular applications of a fertilizer high in nitrogen will keep the leaves healthy.

Temperature and humidity Because it originates in the tropics, it does not tolerate very cold weather and needs warmth to maintain good health. Humidity is essential and can be achieved by spraying the air around the plants or by placing containers filled with water among them. The humidity will increase as the water evaporates.

General care New side growth can be cleanly cut away and replanted in moist sand.

Pests and diseases Mealy bugs (see page 33).

Anthurium spp.
Flamingo flower

Aphelandra squarrosa
Zebra plant

Anthurium andraeanum (shown above), the most popular species, has been used to produce many hybrids. The large leaves are dark green and the pink or red flower heads have a shield-shaped spathe with a cream spadix. *A. scherzeranum* has a more compact growth with smaller leaves and a rounded spathe, which surrounds a strangely curled spadix. *A. andraeanum* is grown to a large extent as a cut flower, while *A. scherzeranum* is more suitable as a house plant.

Light This plant prefers deep or semi-shade, or filtered light with good air circulation.

Soil and water The soil should be rich and friable and made up of a mixture of compost, sand, well-rotted manure and charcoal, allowing water to flow through freely. Water lightly but regularly. The addition of a top dressing of compost twice a year will provide the plant with sufficient nutrients.

Temperature and humidity *Anthuriums* thrive in hot, humid conditions. The leaves and surrounding air can be mist-sprayed in hot weather and the pot can be placed on (not in) a bed of wet pebbles to keep up humidity. These plants must be given warmth and shelter in winter.

General care Long stems should be cut back. These cut sections can be left to dry out for a day or two to prevent the stem from rotting, and can be replanted in clean, coarse sand.

Pests and diseases Scale, mealy bugs and red spider mites (see page 33).

This is a fairly recent addition to the house plant world. It is a striking plant with shining, leathery dark-green leaves with prominent white veins. The leaves are attractive on their own but the plant also bears flowers of clear gold, which are borne on sturdy, upright stems.

Light Strong light is necessary for the development of the flowers and a little morning sun can be tolerated. A free flow of air is esssential but there should be no draughts as this could damage the leaves.

Soil and water The soil should be made up of loam, compost and sand, with pot-plant food added to the mixture – this will allow a strong root system to develop. Watering should be frequent from late spring through to late summer, with weekly applications of pot-plant food or weak liquid manure. In winter, food and water should be cut down.

Temperature and humidity Originating in South America, this plant needs warmth and a humid atmosphere. It does not tolerate frosty conditions.

General care As soon as the flowers die they should be removed and the stem cut back to a pair of strong, healthy leaves. Tip cuttings can be taken and these will grow easily if planted in clean, coarse sand.

Pests and diseases Red spider mites (see page 33).

Ardisia crispa
Coral berry

Asparagus densiflorus 'Myersii'
Cat's tail fern

This lovely plant from Asia resembles a small tree. It has a sturdy central stem bearing shiny, dark-green leaves and white or pink flowers, which give way to clusters of coral red berries. It can be grown outdoors on a covered patio in frost-free areas, but should be kept as an indoor plant in colder regions.

Light It must have strong light with morning sun and a free circulation of air.

Soil and water Soil that is rich in compost and has good drainage will encourage growth. Regular watering (a good drenching once a week) during the growing season (late spring to early autumn) will keep it healthy, as will an application of fertilizer every three to four weeks from late spring through summer.

Temperature and humidity Thriving as it does in sub-tropical conditions, this plant does not tolerate extreme cold. It can survive the winter if food is cut out from autumn, and watering is kept to a minimum. This will prevent any new growth which could be damaged by the cold.

General care If growth becomes too spindly the main stem can be cut back in early spring. The seeds can be grown in trays of clean sand mixed with a little compost, and should be kept in a sheltered position.

Pests and diseases Seldom attacked.

Often mistaken for a fern, and even called an asparagus fern, this is actually a member of the lily family and bears seeds, not spores. The short, needle-like leaves are borne on long stems and form a green cylinder. It is best planted in a tall pot or hanging basket to allow the stems to cascade freely.

Light This plant needs strong, filtered light and can even tolerate a little morning sun.

Soil and water The soil should be mixed with loam and compost. From spring, when the new growth is visible, the plant should be watered sparingly at first, and later given a good drenching once a week. Fertilizer high in nitrogen will encourage healthy foliage. In winter water should be reduced to a minimum until new spring growth is evident.

Temperature and humidity This plant does not need extra humidity but should be kept moist during its growing season (spring to autumn). It can tolerate low temperatures.

General care The root clumps should be divided in autumn (see page 23), but take care not to damage the fleshy tuberous roots.

Pests and diseases Seldom attacked.

Asparagus densiflorus 'Sprengeri'
Sprenger asparagus fern

Aspidistra elatior
Cast-iron plant

This *Asparagus* is indigenous to South Africa. It has long, arching stems of closely packed leaves, and bears a mass of small creamy flowers followed by bright red berries. It dies down in winter. With its cascading fronds, it is suitable for hanging baskets or for planting in tall containers.

Light It needs strong light and will tolerate morning sun.
Soil and water The soil mixture should be made up of loam, compost and a little coarse sand. From early spring encourage new growth with water, and later with regular applications of liquid manure. Stop feeding during winter and keep the soil moist, but not wet, until spring.
Temperature and humidity This plant prefers warm growing conditions. It will thrive in normal conditions with no extra humidity as long as it is watered regularly.
General care Divide root clumps in spring (see page 23).
Pests and diseases Seldom attacked.

ASPARAGUS vs PROTASPARAGUS

At one time, when referring to *Asparagus densiflorus* 'Myersii' and *Asparagus densiflorus* 'Sprengeri', the name *Asparagus* was changed to *Protasparagus*. Today however, it is once more known as *Asparagus*.

The *Aspidistra* is a hardy, easy-to-grow plant, which unfailingly produces a harvest of handsome leaves. It forms compact rosettes of dark-green, wide leaves rising straight from the earth, and sometimes produces small, dark flowers from the base of these leaves. A variegated form is also available.

Light This plant grows in deep shade or semi-shade and does not tolerate direct sunlight.
Soil and water It needs a soil mix of loam and compost, with sand and charcoal added for good drainage. When the plant comes into new growth in spring, it can be encouraged with regular watering and feeding with a liquid manure or special foliage plant food.
Temperature and humidity It prefers cool conditions but can tolerate limited periods of heat or extreme cold. Extra humidity is not necessary if the plant is watered regularly.
General care Only divide clumps (in spring) if the plant is overcrowded (see page 23).
Pests and diseases Scale, mealy bugs and red spider mites (see page 33).

Asplenium nidus
Bird's nest fern

Aucuba japonica 'Variegata'
Spotted laurel / Gold dust plant

This unusual but popular indoor plant forms a rosette of broad, bright-green leaves, which have slightly undulating margins and a midrib of black. As the leaves mature they become coarse and leathery. The leaves can grow to a metre or more in length, but if the plant is kept in a small pot the growth can be restricted.

Light This fern needs strong, filtered light but no direct sun, and must have a good circulation of fresh air which is free of draughts.

Soil and water A loose, aerated soil mix with good drainage is essential. During the growing season (spring to autumn) it should never be allowed to dry out completely. Weak liquid manure or special fern food should be given every two weeks, followed by a thorough watering. Water can also be poured into the centre of the leaf rosette.

Temperature and humidity It needs both warmth and humidity and its leaves should be mist-sprayed during hot, dry weather.

General care The plant should be placed in an area where the leaves cannot be damaged by passers-by.

Pests and diseases Scale and mealy bugs (see page 33).

Aucubas were very popular with the Victorians, who cherished them for their shining green leaves and their ability to grow almost anywhere. 'Variegata' has leaves of bright green with a sprinkling of gold, and forms a neat, compact shrub. The flowers are very small and will only develop into scarlet berries if a male and female plant are placed close together.

Light Strong light with a little morning sun is best. It does tolerate poor light but this will cause the leaves to lose their colour.

Soil and water Soil with good drainage is essential. Watering should be moderate throughout the growing season (spring to autumn) and should be cut down in winter.

Temperature and humidity Although it tolerates cold, this plant does much better in room temperature conditions. Humidity should be increased in hot weather by spraying the leaves with a fine mist.

General care Prune back woody or straggling growth in autumn or spring.

Pests and diseases Scale (see page 33).

Beaucarnea recurvata
(*Nolina recurvata*)
Ponytail / Elephant foot tree

Begonia eliator
No common name

This is an unusual plant which is used to desert conditions (it originates in Mexico) and has the ability to store water in its enlarged stem base. It is easy to grow as long as it is not over-watered and has good drainage. Arched spikes of small yellow flowers may appear in spring. This plant will probably be a talking point and should be placed on its own as a feature.

Light This plant requires strong light and will thrive if allowed direct sun for part of the day.

Soil and water The soil mix should be extremely well drained and should have coarse sand or charcoal added to it. Fertilizer should be applied once a month, followed by a good watering. Great care must be taken not to over-water the plant as this will rot the roots and stem – a thorough soaking once every two weeks is sufficient.

Temperature and humidity With its ability to store water this plant can withstand drought conditions. However, it cannot tolerate extreme cold and should be moved away from windows during the winter months.

General care Great care should be taken to ensure that the roots are never allowed to become waterlogged, especially during winter.

Pests and diseases Seldom attacked.

This attractive plant is valued for its flowers, which bloom in spring and range from white through pink to orange and almost scarlet. The flowers are borne on brittle stems that can snap easily. The dark-tinted leaves have an attractive rounded form.

Light The light should be strong and the plant can tolerate a little morning sun. Poor air circulation could encourage the growth of mildew, which can also be caused by surplus water on the leaves.

Soil and water The fibrous roots need a firm soil, rich in compost and loam, to provide suitable anchorage. The plant should be kept damp from spring when new growth appears. As soon as new growth is well established, a programme of regular feeding with a suitable fertilizer should be carried out until autumn. After this, watering should be cut down to allow the plant a winter rest.

Temperature and humidity If the air becomes dry, the buds may drop. To obviate this, the pot can be sunk into a larger container of peat moss or can be set on top of wet pebbles.

General care This plant will need to be supported from its early stages (see pages 31–32).

Pests and diseases Powdery mildew (see pages 32–33).

Begonia rex
Rex begonia

Begonia Tuberhybrida hybrids
Hybrid tuberous begonias

One of the most spectacular foliage plants, the Rex begonia comes in a vast range of colours and colour combinations in leaves that are large and slightly pleated. Care must be taken with these plants as the stems are extremely brittle and the leaves damage easily. These colourful plants are best suited to shallow containers.

Light This plant needs bright light, but no direct sun. They will grow in fairly deep shade but the colour of the leaves will deteriorate under these conditions.

Soil and water The soil should be rich and friable. During the growing season (spring to autumn) the plant should be kept moist (not soggy) and should be given regular doses of liquid fertilizer.

Temperature and humidity Artificial heat and stuffy conditions can cause the leaves to dry out. Humidity during the growing season is essential.

General care The rhizomes can be divided in spring and leaf cuttings can be taken (see pages 24–25).

Pests and diseases Powdery mildew (see pages 32–33).

From an insignificant tuber will arise a plant with handsome leaves, followed by beautiful flowers ranging in colour from white to glowing crimson, orange and yellow, with gentle pink in between. Male and female flowers are borne on the same plant, with the female flowers taking a single form. Unless seed is to be collected, the female flowers should be removed as soon as they die to allow for strong new growth.

Light Strong light with a little morning sun is essential.

Soil and water The soil mix should be made up of equal parts of compost and loam, with 5 ml (1 teaspoon) each of bone meal and plant food added to it. Pour the water around and not on top of the tuber, which should be placed only half submerged on the surface. Watering can be sparse until the new leaves are well developed. Thereafter, water heavily and regularly, with weekly applications of plant food.

Temperature and humidity Warm growing conditions are necessary and the plants should be given extra humidity during hot, dry weather.

General care After flowering, allow the leaves to die down gradually. Remove the top growth and store tubers in a cool, dry place. The tubers (concave side up) can also be grown in trays of sand and the new stems can be used as cuttings. As the stems are extremely brittle, plants should be supported as soon as the stem is 10 cm (4 in) tall (see pages 31–32).

Pests and diseases Powdery mildew (see pages 32–33).

Billbergia nutans
Queen's tears

Browallia speciosa
Bush violet

An old favourite for many years, this plant has been among the most popular of the bromeliads because it is so easy to grow. Its masses of pale green leaves form a tight rosette and from this arises a slender stalk with attractive pink bracts enclosing green and purple flowers.

Light The light should be strong and there should be a good circulation of air around the plant.

Soil and water The soil should be sandy and should have bark chips or charcoal added to it to ensure good drainage. The leaves form a tight rosette with a central 'tank', which should be filled with water at all times. Regular (once every ten days) applications of fertilizer followed by a thorough drenching will keep the plant healthy.

Temperature and humidity Any sudden drop in temperature should be avoided. Hot, dry conditions could cause leaves to turn brown but this can be obviated by regular misting of the leaves and surrounding air.

General care New plantlets growing from the main plant can be cleanly cut away and replanted in clean, coarse sand (see page 25).

Pests and diseases Scale (see page 33).

This small plant has a shrubby growth and bears a mass of blue or white tubular flowers from spring through to late autumn. This is not a spectacular plant but it is charming when placed in a bowl on a low table, or when several are planted together in a communal container.

Light Strong light is essential and a little morning sun is allowed.

Soil and water The soil mix should have good drainage. Generous watering, especially during hot weather, should be given once a week and a little fertilizer should be added as the first buds appear to ensure a good blooming.

Temperature and humidity This plant needs high humidity. It does not tolerate very cold weather and it is best to discard it at the end of the season and acquire new plants for the following spring.

General care To keep the plant compact and bushy, new growth should be pinched out from the tips and any dead or weak growth should be cut away. The plants will die back and flowering will cease as winter approaches. The seed can be collected and sown in trays (see page 24), which should be kept in a sheltered place. Tip cuttings can also be taken in autumn or spring (see page 25).

Pests and diseases Red spider mites (see page 33).

Caladium bicolor (*C. hortulanum*)
Angel wings

Calathea makoyana
Peacock plant

This popular house plant displays spectacular colour and veining in its leaves, which last from spring through to autumn. However, it dies down completely in winter. Planted in groups in large containers, *Caladiums* make a spectacular display of colour for many months.

Light The light should be strong but direct sunlight and draughts should be avoided. These plants will grow in shady conditions but their colour will suffer.

Soil and water The soil should be enriched with compost or well-rotted manure. At the first signs of renewal, the plant should be given only water. Once the leaves have unfurled, weak liquid manure can be applied weekly, followed by a good watering.

Temperature and humidity This plant should be given warmth during the growing season (spring to autumn) and extra humidity in hot, dry weather.

General care When the leaves have died down completely, cut them off and store the tubers in a dry place until spring.

Pests and diseases Seldom attacked.

This plant, originating in the warm and humid rain forests of Brazil, bears large, oval leaves which are heavily veined in darker colours. The leaves are borne on straggling stems and are well displayed to receive light.

Light The light should be strong, with no direct sunlight. It can tolerate low light for short periods.

Soil and water The soil mix should be loose and friable and allow water to run through freely. The plant should be watered regularly and leaves can be sprayed with a fine mist. Special foliage food can be given but take care not to apply any to the leaf surfaces as this could damage them. Water and food can be cut down in winter and gradually increased again from early spring.

Temperature and humidity This plant relishes warm, damp conditions and will suffer if there is a sudden drop in temperature during the growing season (spring to autumn). A tray of water placed near the plant will help keep up humidity as the water evaporates.

General care If the root clump has crowded its pot it should be divided in late winter or early spring (see page 23).

Pests and diseases Mealy bugs and red spider mites (see page 33).

Callisia repens
No common name

Capsicum annuum
Ornamental pepper

This low-growing plant has divided, spreading stems, which bear a multitude of small green leaves with purple undersides. The leaves become dark purple in autumn and winter. *Callisias* are ideal for both small or large containers, and can also be planted in hanging baskets due to their cascading nature.

Light Strong light is essential and a little direct sun for part of the day will encourage healthy growth.

Soil and water The soil should have good drainage and fertilizer should be applied sparingly. A thorough watering once a week is vital.

Temperature and humidity Coming as it does from South America, this plant needs warmth and humidity and should be sprayed during hot, dry weather.

General care Pinch out the growing tips regularly to maintain a compact shape.

Pests and diseases Seldom attacked.

These small, shrubby plants produce shining red, purple or orange fruits, some being long and pointed, others round. They are produced from early summer and are long-lasting, making this a colourful plant for any part of the house. It should be regarded as an annual and seeds can be planted in spring for a summer blooming. Ideal Christmas decorations, the fruit-bearing plants can be placed throughout the house.

Light They need strong bright light all through the day, with direct sun for part of the day.

Soil and water The soil should have good drainage to allow the water to flow through freely. Take care not to over-water the plant – once every ten days should be sufficient.

Temperature and humidity This warm-climate plant will thrive in a warm, sunny spot. Humidity should be controlled as the plant does not tolerate constant moisture.

General care Pinch out the new terminal growth for a neat, compact bush. The fruits have a typical hot taste and the plants should be placed out of reach of children who may be tempted to eat the brightly coloured peppers.

Pests and diseases Seldom attacked.

Ceropegia linearis ssp. *woodii*
Sweetheart vine

Chamaedorea elegans
Parlour palm

This plant originates in South Africa and in its natural habitat can often be seen hanging from rocks or branches. The small, heart-shaped leaves are slightly succulent and are borne on slender, trailing stems which give rise to small, unusual flowers. This endearing plant is easy to grow and a large plant can survive in a fairly small container.

Light This plant need strong light, with direct sun for part of the day.

Soil and water The soil mix should include ordinary garden soil and compost. Watering should not be overdone as there is a danger of rotting and the plant should only be fed once a month during the growing season (spring to autumn).

Temperature and humidity It tolerates most adverse conditions except extreme cold. Extra humidity is not necessary.

General care If the plant takes on a straggling look it is best to cut back the trailing stems to a few centimetres to encourage new growth. The cut sections of the stem can be replanted in clean, moist sand.

Pests and diseases Seldom attacked.

This attractive palm has a single stem with feathery leaves and may produce sprays of flowers followed by fruit at an early age. It has a good shape when very young. Miniature palms in tiny pots make wonderful gifts.

Light This plant needs strong light, but no direct sun.

Soil and water The soil mix should be rich and friable, with an extra layer of rocks at the bottom of the container to ensure good drainage. Although the plant does not like to dry out completely, it does not tolerate water around its roots. In winter, water should be cut down gradually.

Temperature and humidity Warm conditions and normal humidity levels will encourage healthy growth. A sudden drop in temperature may cause the leaves to turn brown at their edges.

General care Keep the plant out of draughts and ensure that it does not become waterlogged.

Pests and diseases Scale, mealy bugs and red spider mites (see page 33).

Chamaedorea seifrizii
Reed palm

Chlorophytum comosum
Hen and chicken

With its dark green stems and leaves, this popular palm creates clumps of stems and can grow as tall as two metres under good conditions.

Light It will grow in fairly deep shade or in stronger light, but does not tolerate direct sun.

Soil and water The soil mix must be rich, friable and have good drainage. The palm should be given plenty of water during summer.

Temperature and humidity This plant does not tolerate cold conditions and should be moved to a warm position during winter. Extra humidity is not necessary.

General care To maintain an attractive appearance, cut any old woody stems down to the ground to encourage new growth. The plant may eventually grow too large for its container, in which case the new stems can be cut away from the main plant and replanted in separate pots.

Pests and diseases Scale and mealy bugs (see page 33).

This popular house plant has green-and-white striped leaves, which are narrow and curved and form a neat, compact shape. The common name is derived from the plant's habit of sending out long, arching stems that give rise to small new plants at their tips, and surround the mother plant with a 'basket' of stems. These plants can be grown in a pot or hanging basket.

Light The plant should be placed in strong light.

Soil and water The soil can be a commercial potting mix or a mix of loam, compost and sand with the addition of plant food. Water should be generously applied, especially during hot weather.

Temperature and humidity Warmth and humidity are essential to healthy growth and sudden drops in temperature should be avoided.

General care Dead or damaged leaves should be cut out regularly to maintain a neat appearance. The small new plants at the ends of the arching stems can be cut away and planted into separate pots. Clumps can be divided in spring (see page 23).

Pests and diseases Seldom attacked.

Chrysalidocarpus lutescens
Golden yellow palm

Clivia miniata
Flame of the forest

This is one of the most popular palms for both indoor and outdoor cultivation. It has multiple stems of golden-yellow and yellow-green leaves with a golden midrib. The scars left by old leaves are an added attraction.

Light This palm needs strong light with a little morning sun during summer.
Soil and water The soil should be loose and friable and have good drainage. Although the plant requires frequent watering during summer, it should never be allowed to become waterlogged. In winter, water can be cut down.
Temperature and humidity As this plant comes from the tropics, it needs warmth and humidity. It should be protected in winter as it does not tolerate sudden drops in temperature.
General care To maintain a neat appearance the leaves should be wiped clean regularly with a soft, damp cloth.
Pests and diseases Scale, mealy bugs and red spider mites (see page 33).

For many years this South African plant has been valued as a house plant. The flowers are usually orange in colour, but cream and yellow varieties are also available. These handsome plants will brighten up any corner of the room.

Light *Clivias* need semi- or deep shade, but no direct sun.
Soil and water The soil mix must be rich in compost and leaf mould and should have sand added to it for good drainage. Watering should be generous from spring through to autumn, but should be cut down in winter.
Temperature and humidity Although it is a sub-tropical plant, it should not be subjected to extreme heat. Humidity is essential in hot, dry weather.
General care They should be allowed to grow unchecked in large containers for several years before the clumps are divided (see page 23).
Pests and diseases Mealy bugs (see page 33).

Codiaeum hybrids
Croton

Coffea arabica
Coffee plant

Codiaeums are renowned for their brilliantly coloured foliage. The colours range from pink to maroon and from pale gold to orange, with different shades of green in-between. The leaves also have a variety of shapes, making these plants an invaluable addition to any indoor display. They can even be grown outdoors in warm, frost-free gardens.

Light To develop their full colour, these plants must have plenty of light, even direct sunlight, for part of the day. Poor light will deteriorate leaf colour and draughts can damage the leaves.

Soil and water The soil should have good drainage and watering should be copious from late spring through to autumn. General fertilizer can be given in small quantities.

Temperature and humidity As these are tropical plants they must be protected from the cold. *Codiaeums* do not tolerate sudden temperature changes, which will cause the leaves to drop, and may prove difficult to grow where temperature fluctuations occur.

General care The leaves should be cleaned regularly to maintain an attractive appearance.

Pests and diseases Scale, mealy bugs and red spider mites (see page 33).

This has proved to be a highly successful indoor plant. It is a shrub with a dense growth of dark-green leaves and fragrant white flowers, which may give way to coffee beans if the growing conditions are suitable.

Light It will grow in fairly deep shade but will do better in semi-shade, with no direct sun.

Soil and water The soil should be enriched with compost and have good drainage. Give the plant a thorough drenching once a week.

Temperature and humidity It needs warm, humid growing conditions. It can be grown in air-conditioned rooms but will suffer in very dry conditions. The leaves should be sprayed in hot, dry weather.

General care Nip back new terminal growth to prevent a straggling look. Although it is interesting to produce your own coffee beans, it is best to enjoy the flowers and then remove them so that the growing beans do not take too much nutrition from the plant.

Pests and diseases Scale, mealy bugs and red spider mites (see page 33).

Columnea microphylla
Column flower

Cordyline fruticosa 'Cream'
No common name

This popular plant always creates a talking point when it is in full bloom. The long, trailing stems covered with oval leaves and scarlet tubular flowers are shown to their best advantage when planted in a hanging basket.

Light The light should be strong and there should be a good circulation of air around the plant.

Soil and water This plant needs a rich, friable soil that will allow the water to run through freely. It will die down in winter, when it requires the minimum of watering.

Temperature and humidity Warm, humid conditions are essential for healthy growth. The air surrounding the plant can be mist-sprayed during hot, dry weather to increase humidity levels.

General care The flowers should be removed as soon as they die and in spring new stems can be cut back for a more compact, neater growth.

Pests and diseases Red spider mites (see page 33).

There are many outstanding varieties of *Cordyline fruticosa*, most of them in shades of pink, burgundy and cerise, with occasional green. The 'Cream' variety has long, narrow variegated leaves of cream and green.

Light The light should be strong to preserve the leaf colours. A few hours of direct sun each day will be beneficial to the plant.

Soil and water A rich and friable soil with good drainage is essential. Water should only be given when the soil's surface is dry and during winter it can be cut down until the soil is only slightly moist.

Temperature and humidity These plants should be moved to a warm position during winter. The leaves should be sprayed with a fine mist during hot weather to prevent them from drying out.

General care If the plant becomes too long and leggy, the top growth can be removed and planted in clean, coarse sand in a separate container. The original stem will put out new side growth which can be left as it is or used for cuttings (see page 24–25).

Pests and diseases Red spider mites (see page 33).

Cordyline fruticosa glauca
No common name

Cryptanthus hybrids
Earth star

Cordylines, often mistaken for *Dracaenas*, are highly prized for their vividly coloured leaves borne on slender central stems. *C. f. glauca* has a dense growth of fairly broad, emerald-green leaves. The plant has a more compact growth than most *Cordylines*. There are also other varieties of *C. fruticosa* – enquire at your local nursery to find out what is available.

Light This plant needs strong light with a good circulation of air but no draughts.

Soil and water A mix of well-rotted compost and a loose and friable commercial potting soil is essential. Plenty of water and applications of weak liquid manure every three or four weeks during the growing season (spring to autumn) will keep this plant healthy.

Temperature and humidity Warmth and humidity are important. During hot, dry weather the leaves should be wiped with a damp cloth.

General care If the plant becomes too tall and straggly it should be cut back. The cut piece can be replanted in clean, coarse sand.

Pests and diseases Red spider mites (see page 33).

These terrestrial bromeliads are well named as they grow close to the earth, forming star-like rosettes of broad, lustrous leaves with undulating margins. They bear small, short-stemmed, creamy flowers.

Light Partial shade is ideal, with no direct sunlight.

Soil and water The soil should be mixed with stones, pine-bark chips or vermiculite to ensure good drainage. The plant can be kept in good health by keeping the leaf 'tank' filled with water, and it should be given regular applications of special foliage plant food or liquid manure every ten days or two weeks.

Temperature and humidity This plant needs warmth and humidity and does not tolerate cold. To keep up humidity, and an attractive appearance, the containers can be placed on wet pebbles.

General care Warm growing conditions are essential for these attractive bromeliads which, when grouped together, make a spendid display.

Pests and diseases Scale and mealy bugs (see page 33).

Ctenanthe oppenheimiana '*Tricolor*'
Never-never plant

Cyclamen persicum
Florist's cyclamen

This is an evergreen plant with leathery leaves borne on slender stems and forms a low, dense mass of growth. The undersides of the leaves are wine coloured, while the green upper surface is striped with silver. They make a striking addition to any group of house plants.

Light Strong light, but no direct sun, is necessary for strong colouring in the leaves.

Soil and water A rich and friable soil, with generous watering in the growing season (spring to autumn) and monthly applications of special foliage plant fertilizer, will encourage healthy growth.

Temperature and humidity As it comes from a warm and tropical climate, this plant does not tolerate low temperatures. It needs warmth and humidity all through the year.

General care Straggling and untidy stems can be cut back to encourage new growth.

Pests and diseases Seldom attacked.

This exquisite plant has the advantage of flowering in winter. The heart-shaped leaves in shades of green and silver are an attraction in themselves and are borne on sturdy stems. The white, pink, red or purple flowers have glistening reflexed petals, often with a darker shade at the centre.

Light This plant needs strong light with a little morning sun. It should be placed in a position free of draughts.

Soil and water The soil should be rich in compost and have good drainage. Water should never be applied over the corm or leaves – some growers prefer to place the pot in a dish of water rather than risk rotting the corm.

Temperature and humidity This plant does well in a cool atmosphere with extra humidity.

General care After flowering, the plant will start to die down and watering should be cut down gradually until all the leaves are yellow. At this stage, place the pot on its side in a cool, dry place until autumn. New growth should be encouraged by regular watering. When the leaves are well developed, fertilizer should be applied.

Pests and diseases Botrytis (grey mould) (see page 32).

Cymbidium hybrids
Boat orchid

Dieffenbachia amoena
Dumb cane

One of the most popular orchids among amateur growers, these *Cymbidiums* have a strong growth of strap-like leaves and give rise to firm flowers borne along the length of each arching stem. The flowers are long-lasting and the plants are often grown in greenhouses and then brought indoors during flowering.

Light *Cymbidiums* need bright light, but no direct sun, when in flower, and should be placed in a well-ventilated position.
Soil and water Special orchid soil mixes are available from nurseries or you can make up your own mix with charcoal and pine-bark chips added to it to ensure good drainage. The plants should be freely watered during the growing season (summer) and should be sprayed in hot weather. Regular feeding with special fertilizer is also necessary.
Temperature and humidity *Cymbidiums* need warm growing conditions, but cooler night temperatures are essential.
General care If the plant has filled its pot it should be repotted immediately after flowering (see page 23).
Pests and diseases Scale, mealy bugs and red spider mites (see page 33).

This plant was given the name 'dumb cane' because the sap, if it gets onto your tongue, can render you speechless for some time. It is a striking plant with large leaves in various shades of green. It makes a splendid indoor feature and can be grown outdoors in sub-tropical regions. Because it is poisonous, it should be placed where children cannot reach it.

Light This plant should be kept in light shade. It can survive for short periods in deep shade but this will lead to straggling growth.
Soil and water The soil mix should be rich in organic material – commercial potting soil with the addition of compost is ideal – and should have good drainage. A good watering once a week should be sufficient and the leaves should be sprayed regularly. Once new growth is well established, liquid manure can be given once every three weeks. Watering should be cut down in winter.
Temperature and humidity Warm, humid growing conditions are essential. This plant is frost-tender and should be moved to a warm position in winter.
General care As the stem grows, it should be staked. The plant tends to become untidy as it grows taller because the lower leaves fall off. At this stage the stem can be cut back and the severed section planted upright in clean, moist sand. Remember to wash your hands afterwards.
Pests and diseases Scale and red spider mites (see page 33).

Dizygotheca elegantissima
False aralia

Dracaena curculosa
Gold dust dracaena

This unusual house plant resembles a miniature tree because of its slender central stem with side branches. The leaves are dark green verging on black, and have broadly toothed margins. This plant forms a striking contrast in both form and colour to many other house plants.

Light This plant needs bright, strong light with a little morning sun.

Soil and water The soil should be rich and fertile and have good drainage as waterlogged conditions will soon destroy the plant. Watering should be quite generous during the growing season (spring to autumn), but should be cut down in winter.

Temperature and humidity It thrives in warm conditions, with no sudden drop in temperature.

General care The top growth can be cut back from time to time to create a more compact shape.

Pests and diseases Scale, mealy bugs and red spider mites (see page 33).

Dracaenas usually have strap-like leaves but *D. curculosa* has oval leaves on slender stems. The leaves are green in colour and are dusted with speckles of gold, a combination that will brighten up a shadowy corner.

Light The light should be strong, but this plant is also able to survive in poorly lit conditions.

Soil and water The soil should be enriched with organics and have good drainage. Watering should be moderate from spring to autumn – once every ten days is sufficient. Care must be taken not to allow the soil to become too soggy as this could cause the leaves to drop. In winter the plant should be kept moist.

Temperature and humidity Warmth is essential to this tropical plant. Humidity should be normal.

General care Any damaged leaves should be removed to maintain a neat appearance, and leggy growth can be cut back and used as cuttings (see page 25).

Pests and diseases Seldom attacked.

Dracaena fragrans 'Massangeana'
Corn plant

Dracaena marginata 'Tricolor'
Rainbow plant

This species, with its broad leaves borne on a tall central stem, is among the best known of the *Dracaenas*. It makes a statement with its green leaves decorated with a broad, central gold stripe. These plants are often sold in the form of a tall, bare stem bearing rosettes of leaves at the top, and make striking feature plants. The lower growing form creates a softer effect.

Light The light should be strong, with a little morning sun. It can also tolerate poor light for short periods.
Soil and water The soil should be enriched with organic material and have good drainage. Watering should be copious during the growing season (spring to autumn), with large plants needing a good drenching once a week. In winter, water can be cut down but the soil should be kept moist.
Temperature and humidity Being tropical, this plant does not tolerate extreme cold. Humidity should be normal.
General care The leaves should be cleaned regularly with a soft, damp cloth.
Pests and diseases Seldom attacked.

Dracaenas always attract attention and come in various forms and colours. A relatively new specimen, 'Tricolor' is the most attractive with its narrow leaves of green and yellow margined with dark pink. This plant can grow quite tall (it can reach to nearly 1.8 m/6 ft) but its growth can be restricted if it is kept in a small container.

Light This plant prefers light or dappled shade.
Soil and water The soil should be rich and fertile and have good drainage. This plant should not be over-watered – let the soil dry out before giving it a thorough drenching.
Temperature and humidity Warm and humid growing conditions are essential.
General care Leggy growth can be cut back in spring and the severed pieces can be planted in clean, coarse sand.
Pests and diseases Seldom attacked.

Epiphyllum hybrids
Orchid cactus

**_Epipremnum aureum_
(_Scindapsus aureus_)**
Devil's ivy

The long, flattened green stems can at first appear rather untidy and insignificant but when the buds appear they open to reveal flower heads of creamy white, red, pink or orange. The flowers are surrounded by equally colourful bracts in vivid shades of pink or red.

Light _Epiphyllums_ need strong, filtered light.
Soil and water The soil should be rich and have good drainage. Water should only be given when the soil has dried out completely. They should be watered when the new growing season starts in spring and a low nitrogen fertilizer, such as 2:3:4, should be given once a month.
Temperature and humidity This plant needs warm, humid growing conditions and should be moved to a warm position during cold weather (they are frost-tender).
General care Stem cuttings can be taken in spring or summer and planted upright in clean, coarse sand.
Pests and diseases Scale and mealy bugs (see page 33).

This stunning plant has thick, shining green leaves with flecks of gold, and can be trained to climb a moss stick or other support. It can also be planted in a hanging basket. If properly cared for this is a worthwhile house plant that will live for many years.

Light This obliging plant will grow in strong, bright light or semi-shade.
Soil and water Good quality potting soil with the addition of compost should be adequate. Feed with a special pot-plant fertilizer or liquid manure every five or six weeks. It should be given plenty of water.
Temperature and humidity Warm growing conditions and high humidity are essential.
General care Cut back any weak or straggling stems to maintain a neat appearance.
Pests and diseases Seldom attacked.

Euphorbia pulcherrima
Poinsettia

X Fatshedera lizei
Tree ivy

Through the manipulation of the amount of light they receive, poinsettias can be persuaded to flower at times other than their normal winter flowering time. They have a compact growth and flower at an early age. However, it is the colourful bracts that make these such popular house plants as the flowers themselves are quite insignificant.

Light To keep the bracts colourful, this plant should be given strong light with a little morning sun.

Soil and water The soil must have good drainage and care must be taken not to over-water the plant – it should be allowed to dry out completely before it is given another thorough watering.

Temperature and humidity This plant does not tolerate extreme cold. It should be kept in warm conditions with normal humidity.

General care Because of the special conditions under which potted poinsettias have been cultivated, it is difficult to encourage them to bloom a second time as house plants. However, if they are placed in the garden where the danger of frost is at a minimum, they will grow into a normal bush.

Pests and diseases Mealy bugs and red spider mites (see page 33).

This is a most obliging and versatile plant (produced by crossing a *Hedera* with a *Fatsia*) as it can tolerate adverse conditions for a limited time but will still produce a crop of attractive leaves of green.

Light It needs shade or semi-shade, with a good flow of air around the plant.

Soil and water The soil should be fertile and have good drainage. A good soaking should be given once a week from spring to autumn, and should then be cut down to once every three weeks during winter. Pot-plant food should be added once every two or three weeks in the growing season (spring to autumn).

Temperature and humidity The optimum growing conditions for this plant are a moist and cool atmosphere, but it can tolerate a wide range of temperatures.

General care This plant can either be cut and pinched back to resemble the *Fatsia*, or it can be trained to climb a frame or moss stick. In either form it is a vigorous grower and should be kept in check by judicious clipping back. Cutting the growing tip of the climber will encourage side growth.

Pests and diseases Aphids, scale and red spider mites (see page 33).

Fatsia japonica
Japanese fatsia

Ficus benjamina
Weeping fig

Easy to grow, this *Fatsia* is a handsome plant with large, deeply indented evergreen leaves of dark green. It has a rounded form with dense foliage. Clusters of creamy white flowers are borne in profusion in autumn, giving way to shiny, black berries.

Light The plant should be placed in strong light. It can even tolerate a little direct sun.
Soil and water The soil should be rich and fertile and must have good drainage. It should be kept moist all through the year but should never be allowed to become waterlogged.
Temperature and humidity It can tolerate frosty conditions but prefers warmth and normal humidity. During exceptionally hot, dry weather the plant should be mist-sprayed.
General care If left untouched the *Fatsia* can grow into a large shrub. A good spring pruning will keep it in check and it should be pinched back regularly throughout the year.
Pests and diseases Scale and mealy bugs (see page 33).

Most figs originate from tropical Asia and many have proved to be excellent house plants. *F. benjamina* is probably the most popular and most versatile. It has a mass of small, shining leaves borne on weeping stems. It can grow to 2 m (6 ft 7 in) if planted in a sufficiently large pot. In recent years, the plaited form has proved a great attraction and is created by planting several seedlings in a pot and plaiting them as they grow. The 'lollipop' form, which has a single upright stem bearing dense top foliage clipped into a circular shape, makes an interesting conversation piece.

Light This plant needs strong light and can tolerate direct sun for part of the day.
Soil and water The soil must have good drainage. Watering should be moderate from spring to autumn but should be cut down as winter approaches. A dose of liquid manure every two weeks will keep the plant healthy.
Temperature and humidity It does not tolerate frosty conditions and needs to be protected in winter. Humidity should be high from spring to autumn.
General care The 'lollipop' form should be clipped regularly to maintain its shape.
Pests and diseases Scale and red spider mites (see page 33).

Ficus elastica 'Decora'
India rubber tree

Ficus lyrata
Fiddle-leaf fig

The well-known rubber tree has been a favourite house plant for generations, and rightly so. It is a most obliging plant and can withstand adverse conditions for short periods. Pink bracts enfold the new delicate pink leaves, which unfurl into large, shiny, leathery leaves as they mature.

Light This plant needs strong, bright light, with little or no direct sunlight.

Soil and water The soil should have sand added to it to ensure good drainage, and watering should be moderate. In winter, water should only be given when the soil is dry.

Temperature and humidity This plant thrives in warm, humid growing conditions. Set the pot on wet pebbles or place trays of water around the plant to keep up humidity. The leaves should also be sponged in hot weather. It can tolerate cold but only for a limited time.

General care To avoid tall and gangly growth, cut back the growing tips on the main and side stems.

Pests and diseases Scale, mealy bugs and red spider mites (see page 33).

This striking plant bears the largest leaves of all the fig trees. The leaves are pale green when young but change to dark green as they mature. The plant should be placed on its own as it is inclined to dominate its part of the room.

Light Strong light with a little morning sun is essential.

Soil and water Compost, leafmould and sand should be added to the soil mix to ensure good drainage. A good drenching every ten days from spring to autumn will encourage healthy growth but watering should be cut down in winter to allow the plant to rest.

Temperature and humidity This plant needs warm, humid growing conditions. The leaves should be sprayed in hot, dry weather to keep up humidity.

General care To avoid a leggy, untidy look, the growing tips should be pinched back.

Pests and diseases Scale, mealy bugs and red spider mites (see page 33).

PLEASE NOTE

In their natural state, *Ficuses* can grow into gigantic trees. Do not be tempted to plant them in the garden as foundations, walls and paths will be completely undermined by the invasive roots.

Fittonia verschaffeltii argyroneura 'Nana'
Silver nerve plant (dwarf variety)

Gibasis pellucida (*Tradescantia multiflora*)
Bridal veil

The greatest charm of this small plant is its small, round, emerald-green leaves, which are deeply veined in white. It has a low, spreading growth which shows off its foliage to great advantage. It is best planted in the shallow bowl.

Light It should be placed in a position with strong light but no direct sun.

Soil and water The soil should be enriched with well-rotted compost and should have good drainage. The plant will benefit by being placed in a larger pot of damp soil or compost as the roots are shallow and need to be kept moist. The plant should be watered regularly from spring to autumn, and less frequently during winter.

Temperature and humidity Warm and humid growing conditions are essential.

General care An overall pruning in spring and regular pinching back during the growing season (spring to autumn) will ensure a neat, compact shape.

Pests and diseases Seldom attacked.

This plant is often confused with, and is sometimes sold as, *G. geniculata*. It is, however, a member of the Commelinaceae family. It is not a striking plant but its appeal lies in its delicate, misty appearance, brought about by a multitude of slender stems bearing small white flowers, and dark-green leaves with purple undersides. This is an ideal plant for hanging baskets.

Light It will grow in strong light or semi-shade.

Soil and water A soil mix with good drainage is essential. Watering should be generous from late spring when the new growth appears, but should be cut down to once every two weeks in winter.

Temperature and humidity Normal humidity levels and protection from severe cold will keep this plant healthy.

General care Cut out any untidy or old growth to maintain a neat appearance.

Pests and diseases Seldom attacked.

Guzmania lingulata
Scarlet star

Hedera spp.
Ivy

An epiphytic bromeliad, this plant nevertheless does well in containers. The long, strap-like leaves are pale green and form a rosette with a star-like cluster of crimson bracts in the centre. In spring, stems of brilliantly coloured flowers rise from the centre of the plant. There are many other _Guzmania_ species – enquire at your local nursery to find out what is available.

Light Bright, filtered light is essential.
Soil and water The soil should be very loose, with the addition of pine-bark chips and charcoal to allow the water to flow through freely. The leaves form a 'tank' which should be filled with water at all times. The soil should be kept moist during the growing period (spring to autumn). Cut down water in winter.
Temperature and humidity This bromeliad thrives in a warm and humid atmosphere and does not tolerate cold conditions (it is frost-tender). It should be mist-sprayed in hot, dry weather.
General care New plants may arise from the parent and, when they are about half the size of the parent, they can be removed and planted in separate containers.
Pests and diseases Scale and mealy bugs (see page 33).

Ivy is easy to grow and, being evergreen, is very useful as an indoor plant. Leaves may be large or small, and can be plain green or variegated in gold or silver. Although all ivies will grow indoors, those with the smaller leaves are more suitable as they have a more compact growth. Ivy can be trained to climb a frame, or cascade from a hanging basket.

Light Ivies with variegated leaves will need more light than those species with plain green leaves.
Soil and water The soil should be moderately rich and watering should not be overdone – a good soaking once a week should be sufficient.
Temperature and humidity The plant will remain evergreen if kept in warm conditions. In extreme cold, however, leaves may be damaged or could even drop off, but the plant will recover in warmer weather. The humidity levels should be normal.
General care Damaged or old, woody stems should be cut back in early spring.
Pests and diseases Scale and red spider mites (see page 33).

Hippeastrum hybrids
Amaryllis

Hoya lanceolata
(*H. bella*)
Miniature wax plant

In spring, this large bulb sends up an erect, fleshy stem which produces a head of spectacular trumpet-shaped flowers. The colours of the flowers range from white to red and pink, and some are streaked with white. Although many regard this as a one-off blooming plant, it is possible to keep the bulb for many years.

Light The light should be strong with a little morning sun.
Soil and water The soil should be enriched with organics and have good drainage. After flowering, the leaves will need to be well fed and watered to produce a healthy bulb for the following season. Liquid manure every ten days followed by a good watering will ensure good growth.
Temperature and humidity Warmth is necessary for the bulb to develop. When the leaves are still growing, the humidity should be increased in hot weather.
General care In autumn, growth will slow and food and water can be cut down altogether. Store the dormant bulb in a dry place during winter. In spring it should be planted in rich and friable soil, with half of the bulb showing above the soil surface. Judicious watering will encourage new growth, and when the plant is strong a regular programme of watering and feeding should be started. The flower stem may need support (see pages 31–32).
Pests and diseases Scale and mealy bug (see page 33).

This is an ideal plant for hanging baskets as its dense clusters of wax-like pink or white flowers will be shown to their best advantage. The stems are long and slender and bear fleshy leaves. If planted in a container, it will need support for its climbing stems. The plant should be kept in one place as any sudden change in light or temperature could cause the flowers to drop.

Light Strong light is essential and it can even tolerate an hour or two of direct sun.
Soil and water The soil should have sand and charcoal added to it to ensure good drainage. The plant can withstand dry conditions, but will thrive with moderate watering.
Temperature and humidity Warm and humid growing conditions are essential, and the plant should be sprayed in hot, dry weather.
General care After flowering, the plant can be tidied by cutting back woody and straggling growth.
Pests and diseases Mealy bugs (see page 33).

Hypoestes phyllostachya
Polka dot plant

Impatiens, **New Guinea hybrids**
Busy Lizzie

This little plant has dark-green leaves, speckled with white or even pale or dark pink. They create an informal look in any display of plants and if the different colours of *Hypoestes* are brought together in a large, shallow bowl they will add a splash of colour to a dull corner. It is best to buy young plants as the older ones tend to become quite leggy.

Light They need strong light with a little morning sun. If placed in deep shade their colouring will fade and the stems will become straggly.

Soil and water A potting soil mix with good drainage should be sufficient. The plant should be given a thorough soaking once every seven to ten days.

Temperature and humidity Warmth in the growing season (late spring to autumn) is essential. Extra humidity in the air is not necessary except in extremely dry weather, when the leaves should be sprayed with a fine mist.

General care Pinch out the growing tips to maintain a neat, compact appearance. This plant should be discarded at the end of the season.

Pests and diseases Seldom attacked.

The well-loved busy Lizzie (*Impatiens walleriana*) is appreciated for its flowers which are borne throughout summer. The New Guinea hybrids have leaves of rich and vibrant colours, often with a bronze look. These hybrids have been cultivated to produce flowers that are much larger and of more vibrant colours than those of *I. walleriana*.

Light The light should be strong or filtered, with no direct sunlight except in the morning.

Soil and water The plant needs a rich and friable soil, with plenty of water during the growing season (late spring to early autumn). It will die down in winter and at this time should be given the minimum of water. In spring, the soil can be replenished with pot-plant food and water applied moderately at first, then increasing as the plant grows.

Temperature and humidity *Impatiens* relish warm, humid growing conditions. The leaves should be sprayed in hot, dry weather, but be careful not to spray the flowers.

General care Early growth should be pinched back to create bushy growth. This will also help generate more buds.

Pests and diseases Botrytis (grey mould), aphids and red spider mites (see pages 32–33).

Kalanchoe blossfeldiana
Flaming Katy

Kalanchoe 'Tessa'
No common name

This plant is ideal for bringing colour into the home in late winter and early spring. It is an easy-to-grow succulent with rounded, fleshy leaves that form neat rosettes. The long-lasting red, orange or yellow flowers are borne in clusters at the top of short stalks.

Light This plant must have strong light and can tolerate direct sun.

Soil and water The soil should be enriched with organics and have good drainage. Although *Kalanchoes* are succulents, they do need regular watering throughout spring and summer. A thorough drenching every seven to ten days should be sufficient.

Temperature and humidity This plant does not tolerate frost and will need to be moved to a warm position during the flowering season. Humidity should be normal.

General care This plant often flowers in winter and early spring when temperatures are low. It should not be placed by a window where the leaves could be burnt by the cold.

Pests and diseases Mealy bugs (see page 33).

This is a useful house plant, valued for its leaves as well as for its flowers, which are produced in late winter or early spring. It has an attractive cascading growth that is best displayed in a hanging basket. Its slender stems, with leaves of dark green touched with bronze, produce a mass of small, tubular orange flowers.

Light This plant needs strong light with a little morning sun. It can be placed outside in semi-shade or in a position that receives a little morning sun when all danger of frost has passed.

Soil and water The soil should have good drainage and water should be applied liberally once growth is strong (from spring onwards).

Temperature and humidity This plant does not tolerate frosty conditions and should be moved to a warm position in cold weather. Humidity should be increased in hot, dry weather.

General care If growth becomes straggling and untidy, cut back some of the stems for a more compact shape.

Pests and diseases Mealy bugs (see page 33).

Kentia forsteriana (*Howea forsteriana*)
Kentia palm

Maranta leuconeura
Prayer plant

Its proper name is *Howea* but many people still know it as *Kentia*. This elegant palm has gently arching stems and large leaves. With its graceful height and attractive growth this is one of the most popular indoor palms. However, it might eventually grow too large for its allotted space.

Light This palm tolerates a range of light intensities but should not be placed in direct sunlight. It is ideal for shady corners where few other house plants will grow.

Soil and water The soil should have compost and leaf mould added to it, and extra rocks should be placed at the bottom of the container for good drainage. This plant loves moisture and the leaves should be sponged down during hot weather. The soil should not be wet and soggy in winter.

Temperature and humidity Although it prefers the conditions of its native habitat – that of the warm, humid forest – it does tolerate cool conditions. Trays of water should be placed near the plant and the leaves should be sprayed in hot weather to keep humidity levels constant.

General care The plant should not be placed in a draught or where passers-by can damage the leaves.

Pests and diseases Scale, mealy bugs and red spider mites (see page 33).

This is a beautiful plant with distinctly patterned leaves of velvety green, with pale centres and red veins. Small white flowers spotted with purple appear for a short period during summer. It is called the prayer plant because the leaves stand upright at night.

Light This plant will thrive in a spot where the light is strong and where there are no draughts.

Soil and water The soil should have good drainage to allow regular watering in the growing season (spring to autumn). The plant can be fed every two to three weeks with pot-plant fertilizer, followed by a good watering. Food should be cut out altogether during winter and watering should be minimal.

Temperature and humidity This plant is frost-tender and should be moved to a warm position in winter. Humidity is essential for keeping the large leaves healthy, and the plant should be mist-sprayed or placed in a larger container of moist compost in hot, dry weather.

General care Stems should be cut back when they become untidy. These clippings can be replanted.

Pests and diseases Seldom attacked.

Monstera deliciosa
Delicious monster

Nematanthus gregarius
(N. radicans)
Goldfish plant

This handsome plant has long stems with large, indented and perforated leaves of dark green. It is slow-growing but develops into a very large plant and should be given plenty of space to look its best.

Light The light should be strong, with a little morning sun or filtered sunlight.

Soil and water The soil mix should be enriched with organic material, have good drainage, and be allowed to dry out before more water is applied. Liquid fertilizer should be given once a month in the growing season (spring to autumn).

Temperature and humidity This plant needs warm and humid growing conditions, and should be moved to a warm position during winter. Although it thrives in a humid atmosphere, it can tolerate dry conditions for short periods.

General care When planted indoors it can grow quite tall, but the main stem can be cut back to encourage healthy side growth. The long aerial roots can either be tied to the main stem, or the lower ends can be placed in containers of water, ensuring a constant supply to the plant.

Pests and diseases Scale, mealy bugs and red spider mites (see page 33).

This plant gains its name from the apparent likeness of the flowers to goldfish. It has sturdy stems, shining, dark-green leaves, and tubular orange flowers borne close to the stem. This plant is best suited to bowls and hanging baskets.

Light Strong light will encourage healthy growth and a good harvest of flowers.

Soil and water A friable soil mixed with pine-bark chips will ensure good drainage and allow water to flow through freely. The plant should be given plenty of water when new growth appears in spring, but watering should be cut down in autumn. Care should be taken not to over-feed the plant, as this could cause it to produce few flowers. An application of liquid manure once a month is sufficient.

Temperature and humidity Warm, humid conditions are essential for good growth and flowering.

General care Terminal growth should be pinched back in spring to maintain a neat, compact look.

Pests and diseases Seldom attacked.

Neoregelia hybrids
Blushing bromeliad

**Nephrolepis exaltata
'Boston Gold'**
Boston fern

These plants have the advantage of being able to tolerate cooler conditions better than most other bromeliads. The leaf colour may vary from plain green to variegated stripes or blotches. When the plant flowers, the centre of the leaf rosette will take on a vivid colour. A grouping of different varieties of bromeliads will create an interesting effect.

Light These plants need bright light with a little direct sun to maintain their colour.
Soil and water The soil mix should be rich and friable to allow a free flow of water through the soil. The green leaves form a 'tank' which should always be filled with water. Applications of weak liquid manure every two weeks in spring and summer will keep the plant healthy. Water should be cut down and no fertilizer given in winter.
Temperature and humidity Warmth and humidity are the ideal growing conditions for these plants but they do tolerate cooler conditions.
General care The water in the leaf 'tank' should be changed every three or four weeks.
Pests and diseases Scale and mealy bugs (see page 33).

This Victorian fern, popularly known as the sword fern, is once more coming into favour. 'Boston Gold' is a variety with clear yellow fronds, and is useful for lighting up a shady corner. There are many other varieties – ask at your local nursery or garden centre to find out what is available.

Light This plant will grow in shade or semi-shade.
Soil and water The soil should be rich and friable and have good drainage. With regular watering from spring and fertilizer once every three weeks the fronds will become long and luxuriant.
Temperature and humidity Warm and humid growing conditions are essential. The leaves and air around the plant should be mist-sprayed in hot, dry weather.
General care Old, weak or dead fronds should be removed completely to make way for strong new growth.
Pests and diseases Botrytis (grey mould), whitefly and scale (see pages 32–33).

Pellaea rotundifolia
Button fern

Peperomia caperata
Emerald-ripple pepper

This unusual fern has a spreading rather than upright growth and has round, leathery leaflets borne on short, low-growing stems. It is not a spectacular plant but its dainty growth looks charming if planted in a shallow bowl.

Light This plant will grow in semi-shade or even in a shady, draught-free corner.

Soil and water Gravel and bark should be added to the soil mix to keep it loose and porous. Watering should be frequent during the growing season (spring to autumn) and special fern fertilizer should be applied once a month.

Temperature and humidity This fern tolerates cool conditions and will need to be sprayed in hot, dry weather.

General care This is an evergreen and will need to be kept damp (but not waterlogged) in winter. In spring, old or untidy fronds can be cut back to soil level to make way for strong new growth.

Pests and diseases Scale (see page 33).

Peperomias are available in many varieties, making it a sought-after family of house plants. *P. caperata* has sturdy, pinkish stems, which bear strangely quilted green leaves, and cream flowers that stand proud of the foliage. If planted in a shallow bowl, it will soon spread to make a neat cushion of growth.

Light This plant needs fairly strong light but can also be kept in the shade for short periods.

Soil and water The soil should be enriched with compost or leaf mould and have good drainage – the plant should not be allowed to become waterlogged. Monthly applications of liquid fertilizer should be given in the growing season (spring to autumn).

Temperature and humidity Originating in the tropics, this plant relishes warmth and humidity and does not tolerate sudden drops in temperature.

General care Any damaged or old leaves should be removed by cutting cleanly through the stem at ground level. Allow the plant to fill its container before dividing and repotting (see page 23).

Pests and diseases Seldom attacked.

Peperomia glabella
No common name

Philodendron bipinnatifidum
(*P. selloum*)
Lacy tree philodendron

With its shining, pointed leaves and rambling habit, this *Peperomia* is ideal for both hanging baskets and pots. It is not a spectacular species but is very useful for mixing with other plants in a large container. The unusual flowers resemble slender spikes.

Light The plant should be placed in strong light, with no direct sun.
Soil and water The soil should be mixed with organics and should be friable to ensure good drainage. Water well.
Temperature and humidity Warmth is essential from spring to autumn. There should be no sudden drop in temperature and the plant will need to be moved to a warm position in cold weather. Humidity is necessary to keep the large leaves healthy and in hot, dry weather they can be sprayed with a fine mist.
General care Pinch back the new growth to keep the plant compact.
Pests and diseases Seldom attacked.

This appropriately named *Philodendron* has very large green leaves with ruffled, lace-like edges. This plant will be a welcome addition to any home but should be placed on its own as it can grow very large.

Light The light should be bright, with a little morning sun.
Soil and water The soil mix should be rich in organics and water should be generously applied from spring, then cut down from late autumn to allow the plant to rest.
Temperature and humidity This plant needs warm, humid conditions during the growing season (spring to autumn), and the leaves should be sprayed in hot weather.
General care Stems can be cut back to encourage healthy side growth.
Pests and diseases Seldom attacked.

Philodendron erubescens 'Pink Prince'
No common name

Philodendron scandens
Heart-leaf philodendron

This climbing *Philodendron* has maroon stems with shiny, heart-shaped leaves of dark green with patches of pink. This unusual and interesting house plant will show its beautiful foliage to best advantage if trained to climb a moss stick.

Light This plant must have bright light, with no direct sun.
Soil and water The soil mix should be rich in compost and have good drainage. Soak the plant once a week, and give foliage feed or liquid manure once every two weeks.
Temperature and humidity The temperature should not be allowed to drop too far – room temperature is suitable. In hot, dry weather the humidity should be increased by spraying the leaves and surrounding air with a fine mist.
General care This is a healthy climber and could outgrow its support. If this happens, cut back the terminal growth.
Pests and diseases Seldom attacked.

This *Philodendron* is suitable where space is limited as its neat, heart-shaped leaves are much smaller than other varieties. The slender stems can be trained to twist and climb around a moss stick or other support, creating an attractive dense growth. A variegated form with a gold tinge is also available.

Light The light should be strong, with no direct sun.
Soil and water Commercial potting soil with good drainage should be sufficient. Water should be given weekly from spring to autumn and then cut down to once every two or three weeks in winter.
Temperature and humidity This species can tolerate lower temperatures. The leaves and air surrounding the plant should be mist-sprayed in hot, dry weather.
General care The growing tips should be cut back to prevent woody or leggy growth.
Pests and diseases Seldom attacked.

Phoenix roebelinii
Miniature date palm

Pilea cadierei
Aluminium plant

This palm has gained great popularity because of its attract-ive features and because it is so easy to grow. The slender, rough-barked trunk gives rise to a fountain of dark-green, feathery leaves, and even in its earliest stages it takes on the appearance of a miniature palm. Small yellow flowers give way to black fruits. Another popular palm is _P. dactylifera._

Light This palm tolerates strong light to semi-shade but should have direct sun for part of the day. There should be a free flow of air around the plant.
Soil and water The soil mix should be rich and fertile and have good drainage. Plenty of water should be given in the growing season (spring to autumn) but more sparingly in winter. A weak liquid fertilizer should be given once a month from spring to autumn.
Temperature and humidity Warm, humid growing condi-tions are essential and the plant should be mist-sprayed in hot, dry weather.
General care The leaves should be cleaned regularly with a soft, damp cloth.
Pests and diseases Scale, mealy bugs and red spider mites (see page 33).

This _Pilea_ was given its common name because the leaves look as though they have been dusted with aluminium. In sub-tropical regions this popular plant is often grown as a ground cover, but indoors it should be planted in a shallow container where it can spread and cascade over the edge.

Light This plant should be placed in semi-shade.
Soil and water The soil should be rich in organics and have good drainage. Watering should be generous from spring to autumn – a thorough soaking once a week is sufficient. In winter, cut down watering to once every three weeks.
Temperature and humidity Warm, humid conditions will ensure healthy growth. The pot should be placed on wet pebbles to keep the humidity levels constant.
General care Creeping stems can be pinched back to create compact growth.
Pests and diseases Seldom attacked.

Platycerium bifurcatum
Common staghorn fern

Plectranthus australis
Swedish ivy

This unusual epiphytic fern has two kinds of leaves. One forms large 'shields', which are green and then turn brown as they mature. These leaves help enclose the nutrients that are placed between the shields and the host. The other kind of leaf is in the form of the well-known staghorn. This has become a popular fern, and will grow into a large colony if it is well looked after.

Light It will grow in strong, filtered light or semi-shade.
Soil and water Well-rotted compost should be inserted between the shields and the host plant. It should be given plenty of water in the growing season (spring to autumn). Water should be poured behind the shields.
Temperature and humidity Warmth is essential for healthy growth, as is humidity. Spray the plant and the surrounding air in dry conditions, and place trays of water close to the plant to keep humidity levels constant.
General care Being epiphytic, these ferns will thrive when attached to a tree trunk or piece of wood. The fern can be held in place with a nylon stocking or hessian. It should be tied so that there is space between the shields and host plant for the insertion of food and water.
Pests and diseases Seldom attacked.

The extensive *Plectranthus* family has many striking species. *P. australis* is not a spectacular plant but it is low-growing and tolerates adverse conditions. It is attractive in hanging baskets or flowing over the edge of containers.

Light The light should be strong, with a little direct sun for part of the day. The plant can also be placed in semi-shade.
Soil and water A loose, rich soil with plenty of water and doses of fertilizer every month will keep this plant healthy during the growing season (spring to autumn). It should be allowed a winter rest by cutting down on water.
Temperature and humidity Warm growing conditions are essential from spring to autumn. The leaves should be mist-sprayed in hot, dry weather.
General care New growth can be pinched back to maintain a compact, bushy shape.
Pests and diseases Seldom attacked.

Pleomele reflexa variegata
(*Draceana reflexa*)
Song of India

Polyscias filicifolia
Fern-leaf aralia

This plant is slow-growing and can become very straggly. Despite these drawbacks it makes a beautiful house plant with its attractive reflexed leaves of green and gold.

Light This plant needs strong light, with direct sun for part of the day.

Soil and water The soil mix should be friable, rich in organics, and should have sand added to it for good drainage. The plant should be given plenty of water through to autumn, after which watering should be cut down. Overfeeding could cause leaf edges to turn brown. An application of weak liquid manure once a month is sufficient.

Temperature and humidity It relishes warm and humid conditions, with a rest in winter.

General care Stem tips can be nipped back to encourage new side growth.

Pests and diseases Seldom attacked.

This interesting plant has feathery leaves, which are borne on slender upright stems. It does well outdoors in the tropical garden, and is an attractive feature indoors. It is perfectly suited for planting in an oriental container.

Light The light should be bright, although it will also grow in the shade.

Soil and water This plant must have an enriched, friable soil with good drainage, and generous watering and feeding every three or four weeks.

Temperature and humidity Warm and humid conditions are essential for healthy growth.

General care Untidy or old stems and leaves should be removed in early spring. Sections of the removed stems can be used for cuttings (see page 25).

Pests and diseases Scale, mealy bugs and red spider mites (see page 33).

Pteris cretica 'Albo-lineata'
Cretan brake

Rhapis excelsa
Lady palm

This is a small, sturdy fern with leathery leaves borne on slender stems. The narrow, ribbon-like leaves are green in colour with a central golden stripe, and converge on the stem tip to create an attractive, dense growth.

Light It will grow in bright light or semi-shade.
Soil and water The soil should be loose and friable and enriched with well-rotted compost. Water should be plentiful in summer but cut down in winter. Make sure that the soil does not dry out completely.
Temperature and humidity This cool climate fern should be kept at room temperature conditions. Place the container on wet pebbles to keep up the humidity.
General care Any untidy stems and leaves should be cut down to the soil's surface to make way for new growth. This plant should only be potted on when the container is filled with roots (see pages 22–23).
Pests and diseases Seldom attacked.

This palm forms clumps of stems that are covered with fine dark fibres. Leaves with an unusual, squared-off end are borne in clusters at the end of slender stems. It has several stems that grow close together and give it the appearance of a miniature tropical jungle. It is best placed on the floor to show off the effect of the dense foliage.

Light Although strong light with morning sun is best, this plant will also grow in fairly poor light. It should be kept out of draughts, which could damage the leaves.
Soil and water The soil mix should have sand and compost added to it to ensure good drainage. It should never be allowed to become waterlogged – water should only be given when the soil's surface is dry.
Temperature and humidity This plant tolerates cooler conditions but will need to be moved to a warm position during extremely cold weather. Humidity levels should be increased in hot, dry weather by spraying the plant with a fine mist.
General care Any old or damaged stems should be cut down to ground level to allow younger and stronger growth to develop.
Pests and diseases Scale and mealy bugs (see page 33).

Rhoicissus rhomboidea
African grape

Saintpaulia ionantha
African violet

Also known as grape ivy, this plant climbs by means of coiled tendrils and is valued for its shiny, divided leaves. It will cascade from hanging baskets, but will need a frame or rod for support if it is planted in a container.

Light It should be placed in bright filtered light with no direct sun.

Soil and water The soil should be rich in compost and plenty of water should be given during the growing season (spring to autumn).

Temperature and humidity This plant needs warmth and does not tolerate frosty conditions. The humidity levels should be normal.

General care This fast climber can become untidy if not kept in check by regular pinching back.

Pests and diseases Powdery mildew (see pages 32–33).

African violets are among the most popular flowering house plants, and new colours and forms are constantly being produced. However, this plant probably causes the most distress, for many people complain that their plants suddenly die. 'All they need,' says a leading grower, 'is similar conditions to those which keep us happy – warmth, good light, no draughts and a healthy diet, which, of course, includes water.'

Light This plant thrives in strong light (but no direct sun) and does well under fluorescent lighting.

Soil and water The soil should be rich and fertile and have coarse sand and charcoal pieces added for good drainage. Keep the soil damp and water from the top – do not wet the leaves as droplets could become trapped in the hairs and cause the leaves to rot. Alternate applications of fish emulsion and foliage feed every two weeks.

Temperature and humidity The temperature should remain constant and plants should not become wet and cold or hot and dry. Move them into a warm room in winter.

General care African violets prefer to be slightly rootbound and should only be repotted when the roots have completely filled the pot. Repot between flowering periods and place the plant in a pot of the same size. Simply cut off weak or damaged roots and change the soil.

Pests and diseases Botrytis (grey mould), powdery mildew, whitefly, mealy bugs and red spider mites (see pages 32–33).

Sansevieria trifasciata
Mother-in-law's tongue

Saxifraga stolonifera
Mother of thousands

Despite its unfortunate common name, this is nevertheless an easy-to-grow plant which will tolerate adverse conditions and still look attractive. It can be grown outdoors as well as indoors, and makes a fine show of its slender height. The sword-shaped leaves of *S. trifasciata* have variegated stripes which adds interest.

Light This plant needs strong light with direct sun for most of the day.

Soil and water The soil should have coarse sand and charcoal added to it to ensure good drainage. The plant tolerates dry conditions and does not suffer from being pot-bound; nevertheless if it is given plenty of water from spring it will produce handsome new leaves. Water should be cut down during winter. Young plants should be given monthly applications of liquid manure but established plants will need only one feed during the growing season (spring to autumn).

Temperature and humidity This plant does not tolerate extreme cold. It should be grown at room temperature with normal humidity levels.

General care Any unsightly leaves should be removed immediately. This plant can be divided in spring but only the outer, more vigorous rhizomes should be taken for repotting (see page 23).

Pests and diseases Seldom attacked.

It has been given this name because of the multitude of small new plants that appear at the ends of the pendulous stems arising from the parent plant. The olive-green leaves have a circular shape and are covered with short, stiff hairs. It multiplies quickly and is best planted in a hanging basket or in a shallow bowl placed on a small stand.

Light This plant needs strong light but no direct sun.

Soil and water The soil should be enriched with well-rotted compost and should be friable to ensure good drainage. Water regularly from spring to autumn to ensure that the soil is kept moist but cut down in winter (do not let the soil dry out completely). Feed once a month with commercial pot plant fertilizer or with a weak liquid manure.

Temperature and humidity This plant thrives in cool growing conditions with normal humidity levels.

General care Crowded clumps should be divided in spring and the plantlets at the ends of the stems can be potted into separate pots (see page 23).

Pests and diseases Scale and mealy bugs (see page 33).

Schefflera actinophylla
Umbrella tree

Schefflera arboricola
Miniature umbrella tree

This is one of the most popular and successful house plants. The glossy, green leaves are divided, have a finger-like appearance and are borne on long stalks from a central stem. It is unlikely to flower indoors but as it is evergreen it looks good throughout the year.

Light This plant should be placed in a position with strong light but no direct sun.

Soil and water To maintain luxuriant growth, the soil should be rich in organics and have good drainage. Copious watering and regular feeding during the growing season (spring to autumn) are essential but should be cut down as winter approaches. The soil should never be allowed to dry out completely.

Temperature and humidity This plant tolerates cool growing conditions but prefers a warmer atmosphere with normal humidity. The leaves should be sprayed with a fine mist in hot, dry weather.

General care Cut back the main stem to prevent tall and leggy growth. Terminal growth from side stems can also be cut back for a compact, bushy appearance.

Pests and diseases Seldom attacked.

This species' growth is similar to that of *S. actinophylla* except that it has smaller leaves on a more compact plant. It is also not such a vigorous grower. There are excellent varieties available, including several with gold variations.

Light It should be placed in a position with strong light but no direct sun.

Soil and water To maintain luxuriant growth, the soil should be rich in organics and have good drainage. Copious watering and regular feeding during the growing season (spring to autumn) are essential but should be cut down as winter approaches. The soil should never be allowed to dry out completely.

Temperature and humidity This plant needs to be moved to a warm position in extremely cold weather. Humidity levels should be normal but leaves can be sprayed in hot, dry weather.

General care As the plant grows, it should be staked to keep it upright. Tall and leggy growth should be cut back.

Pests and diseases Seldom attacked.

Sedum morganianum
Donkey's tail

Selaginella kraussiana
Spreading club moss

This quaint and undemanding *Sedum* produces long, drooping stems bearing cylindrical, fleshy grey-green leaves. It is best suited to a hanging basket where its interesting shape will always be the focus of attention.

Light This plant needs bright light, with direct sun for most of the day.

Soil and water The soil mix should have vermiculite or sand added to it for good drainage. Watering should be copious during summer, and special pot-plant fertilizer or liquid manure should be given every five or six weeks.

Temperature and humidity This plant needs protection from the cold. Humidity levels should be normal.

General care Stems that have become long and straggling should be removed at soil level. Plants can be repotted in spring (see page 23).

Pests and diseases Aphids and mealy bugs (see page 33).

This moss-like plant, which spreads its carpet of green growth in shady places, is indigenous to South Africa. It can be placed in its own container or planted under larger plants for a softer effect. Another popular species is *S. k.* 'Aurea', which is pale gold in colour.

Light It is essential that this plant does not get direct sun. Filtered light is best but it also does well in shade.

Soil and water The soil should be porous to allow good drainage, and well-rotted compost should be added to provide extra nourishment. The plant should be watered regularly and the soil should remain moist but not soggy.

Temperature and humidity This plant needs warmth and moisture. Place the container on wet pebbles to keep up humidity levels.

General care Brown and unsightly growth may be seen under the upper green growth. If this appears, shear off the affected patch to make way for new growth. Apply a top dressing of compost and water well.

Pests and diseases Seldom attacked.

Sinningia speciosa
Florist's gloxinia

Soleirolia soleirolii
Baby's tears

This is surely among the most glamorous of house plants with its velvet trumpets of rich and glowing colours. Gloxinias are often received as gifts and are discarded after flowering. However, if properly cared for it is possible to keep this plant for many years.

Light Gloxinias need bright, strong light but no direct sun.
Soil and water A rich and friable soil is essential: add bark and charcoal to ensure good drainage. Water should be applied as a thorough soaking, but the plant should be allowed to almost dry out completely before the next application. Weak liquid manure can be given every two weeks. In autumn the leaves will start to die down, and food and water should be cut out completely.
Temperature and humidity As it is a summer-flowering species, it will thrive in warm conditions. In hot, dry weather, do not spray the leaves but place trays of water close to the plant to allow evaporation to increase humidity levels.
General care When the plant has died down remove the dead leaves and place the pot with the tuber in a cool, dry place for over-wintering. In spring, either replenish the soil or add pot-plant fertilizer. Water sparingly until the new growth appears, then gradually increase the water and food.
Pests and diseases Seldom attacked.

This plant has small, bright-green leaves borne on delicate creeping stems. It is low-growing and spreads very quickly: if planted in a pot or shallow bowl it will soon form a dense mound of growth. It can also be planted at the base of taller plants such as *Aspidistras* or *Dieffenbachias* but its vigorous growth should be kept in check to prevent it becoming too overpowering.

Light It will grow in bright, filtered light or semi-shade.
Soil and water The soil should be enriched with compost and have good drainage. Regular watering is necessary (even once a day in hot weather) as the small leaves dry out quickly. In colder regions this plant dies down in winter, when watering should be cut down to once a week.
Temperature and humidity This plant tolerates a range of temperature and humidity levels but may need to be moved to a warm position in winter as it is frost-tender.
General care Any brown, straggling growth should be removed with a sharp knife. Fill the gaps with compost to encourage new growth.
Pests and diseases Seldom attacked.

Spathiphyllum wallisii
Peace lily

Streptocarpus hybrids
Cape primrose

Easy to grow, this elegant plant with shining leaves of deep green will grow in most places where there is no draught. The creamy white spathes are borne on elegant long stems and gradually change to pale green as they mature.

Light This versatile plant grows in strong light or fairly deep shade.

Soil and water This plant needs plenty of water and a soil mix with good drainage. It is a strong grower and should be given regular applications of foliage feed or liquid manure.

Temperature and humidity It needs warm conditions in the growing season (spring to autumn) and humidity can be kept up by spraying or sponging the leaves in hot weather.

General care Spent flower stems should be removed, as should any dead or unsightly leaves. Clumps can be divided in spring (see page 23).

Pests and diseases Seldom attacked.

Streptocarpus are indigenous to South Africa and many species have large leaves and attractive mauve flowers. The modern hybrids have larger flowers and are available in splendid colours ranging from white through many shades of pink to purple and crimson. Several plants grouped together look outstanding, and one or two placed in a shallow dish will make a superb table centrepiece.

Light The light should be strong, with no direct sun except in the morning. When in bloom, it should be allowed more morning sun.

Soil and water The soil should be rich in organics and have good drainage to allow water to run through freely. Water regularly when new growth appears in spring, and add fertilizer to the water once this growth is well developed. Water should be cut down to a minimum during winter.

Temperature and humidity When in bloom, these plants should not be subjected to extreme heat but humidity levels should be high. To keep up humidity levels, pots can be placed on wet pebbles, or trays of water can be placed among the plants.

General care Spent flowers or leaves should be removed regularly to encourage new growth.

Pests and diseases Mealy bugs (see page 33).

Syngonium podophyllum
Arrowhead plant

Syngonium podophyllum
'Pink Butterfly'
No common name

This plant has leaves which change shape as the plant matures. Young leaves are shaped like an arrowhead, while more mature leaves develop clearly defined lobes. It is a vigorous climber which can be trained up a moss stick, but growth will be slowed if it is planted in a hanging basket. There are some good hybrids, including 'Silver Pearl' and 'White Butterfly', which are not such vigorous climbers.

Light This plant needs strong light with no direct sun.

Soil and water The soil should be enriched with organics and have good drainage as it needs generous watering all through the growing season (spring to autumn). Liquid fertilizer should be applied every two weeks from spring to autumn.

Temperature and humidity Being a warm-climate plant, it does not tolerate extreme cold. Humidity must be high and the plant should be sprayed in hot, dry weather.

General care Growing stems should be cut back regularly to maintain a neat and compact appearance.

Pests and diseases Seldom attacked.

A recent addition to the *Syngonium* family, this charming plant has pointed leaves and leaflets with an unusual glossy sheen of pale pink. It is a climbing plant and can be trained to climb a moss stick or trellis.

Light To maintain leaf colour the light should be strong and the plant can be allowed a little morning sun.

Soil and water The soil should be friable and have compost and pot-plant fertilizer added to it. Water regularly (once a week), giving extra in hot, dry weather. Cut down water in late autumn to give the plant a winter rest. Liquid manure or pot-plant food should be applied every ten days during the growing season (spring to autumn) but should be cut back to once every two or three weeks in winter.

Temperature and humidity Warmth and humidity are essential. This plant does not tolerate frosty conditions and should be protected in winter. Spray the plant in hot, dry weather to keep up humidity.

General care Growing tips should be cut back to create a more compact, bushy shape, and old or damaged leaves should be removed. Stem cuttings can be taken and planted in clean, coarse sand (see page 25).

Pest and Diseases Seldom attacked.

Tradescantia fluminensis variegata (T. albifora)
Wandering Jew

Vriesea splendens hybrids
Flaming sword

Most *Tradescantias* have a trailing habit and leaves of different colours, many of them variegated. *T. fluminensis variegata* has delicate, jointed stems, which bear leaves of differing shades of green. It quickly forms a dense mass of growth and will fill its container to overflowing. A most obliging, easy-to-grow plant for a hanging basket or container.

Light It will grow in bright light with a little morning sun, or in semi-shade.

Soil and water Coarse sand can be added to a commercial potting mix to ensure good drainage. Watering should be increased from the beginning of spring, and fertilizer should be given once a month.

Temperature and humidity This plant needs protection from severe cold and should be given extra humidity from spring to autumn.

General care Dead or untidy stems should be cut back to soil level. Tip cuttings can be taken in spring and planted in moist sand (see page 25).

Pests and diseases Seldom attacked.

This plant is a popular member of the bromeliad family. Its leaves form a rosette and are green in colour with purple-brown bands. The tall flower spike usually appears in mid-summer, and is made up of closely-packed, bright-red bracts that enclose small yellow flowers. The flowers are short-lived but the spike remains colourful for a few months.

Light It should be placed in an area with strong light. A little morning sun will develop the leaf colour and encourage flowering.

Soil and water The soil mix should be loose and friable and have charcoal and sand added to it to allow free drainage. Frequent watering is essential until late autumn when water should be cut down. However, keep the soil damp and the leaf 'tank' filled with water at all times.

Temperature and humidity Warm and humid growing conditions are essential.

General care Coming from a tropical climate, this plant does not tolerate sudden drops in temperature and should be placed in a sheltered position in winter.

Pests and diseases Scale (see page 33).

Yucca elephantipes
Spineless yucca

Zebrina pendula
(*Tradescantia zebrina*)
Wandering Jew

In its natural state, this *Yucca* grows into a large branched plant, but for indoor use the large stems can be cut back to a suitable height. The leaves grow around the cut tip, leaving the rest of the stem bare. Unlike other *Yuccas*, this species' leaves do not have dangerous spikes at their ends. With its stately look and easy maintenance this *Yucca* is highly suited to offices and homes.

Light The light should be strong, with direct sun for most of the day.
Soil and water The soil mix should be made up of one part sand and one part potting soil to ensure good drainage. Give the plant a good watering only when the soil has dried out. A dose of liquid fertilizer or manure every six weeks during the growing season (spring to autumn) should be sufficient.
Temperature and humidity This plant needs warm conditions (it is frost-tender) and can survive long dry periods.
General care Care should be taken not to over-water this plant as this could cause the base of the stem to rot.
Pests and diseases Red spider mites (see page 33).

This plant has been used as a ground cover, pot plant and hanging basket plant for generations because of its vigorous growth and tolerance of adverse conditions. The upper surface of the leaves is variegated in silver and green and the undersides are deep purple.

Light The light should be strong, with a little direct sun each day.
Soil and water A mix of sand and commercial potting soil will ensure good drainage. Watering should be generous, however this plant can tolerate dry conditions for short periods. Feed every six weeks with pot-plant fertilizer, followed by a thorough drenching.
Temperature and humidity Normal humidity and warm growing conditions are essential from spring to autumn.
General care Cut back the stems regularly to maintain a neat and compact shape.
Pests and diseases Seldom attacked.

HOLIDAY CARE

When going on holiday, either for a few weeks or a long weekend, it's best to ask a friend to water and feed your plants while you are away. Clearly explain the watering and feeding requirements of your plants and group those with similar needs to avoid plants being forgotten.

If you cannot find someone to take care of your plants in your absence, there are a few ways of ensuring your plants will be healthy on your return:

- Move plants from windowsills in case of sudden heat waves or cold spells.

- Give all plants a thorough soaking before you leave.

- Place a fertilizer stick or tablet in the soil of those plants that will need to be fed while you are away.

- Small plants can be covered with clear polythene bags: water which is transpired from the plant will condense inside the bag and drip back into the soil.

- Make a temporary wick from water-absorbent material such as an oil lamp wick or a cotton shoe lace. Insert one end through the drainage hole into the soil mix and place the other end in a basin of water.

GLOSSARY

Aerial roots These roots grow above the surface of the soil and are used for climbing and extracting moisture from the air. Commonly found on *Monstera deliciosa*.

Bract A modified leaf which is usually found backing or surrounding insignificant flowers. Normally brightly coloured to attract insects for pollination.

Bud Immature leaf, shoot or flower, which is protected by overlapping scales.

Bulb A storage organ containing a young plant and usually found below ground.

Cactus A succulent bearing spines.

Corm A thick underground stem used for propagation.

Cutting A section of a leaf, stem or root that is used for propagation.

Damping off The death or decay of seedlings caused by over-watering or a fungal infection.

Dead-heading The removal of dead or faded flowers.

Division A method of propagation for perennial plants where the rootball is split into two or more sections.

Epiphyte A non-parasitic plant which grows on another plant and takes nourishment and moisture from the air. Many bromeliads are epiphytic.

Evergreen A plant that retains its leaves all through the year.

Exotic Refers to plants that have been introduced from abroad, usually from the tropics and sub-tropics. Most house plants are exotics.

Family A term which is used to describe a large group of plants with similar characteristics.

Fibre cement A material made up of cement and various organic fibres. It used to be known as asbestos cement but, due to the health hazard, asbestos is no longer used in the manufacture of this product. Often used to make plant containers.

Frond The leaf of a fern or a palm.

Frost-tender Susceptible to damage if the sap freezes.

Fungicide A chemical formulation used to prevent or destroy fungal infections.

Growing point The tip of a shoot where new growth develops.

Hardy Can tolerate frost.

Hybrid The result of crossing two different species.

Inflorescence A grouping of two or more flowers on a single stem.

Inorganic fertilizer A fertilizer developed from a non-living source.

Leaf The area where photosynthesis takes place.

Leaflet A leaf-shaped section of a compound leaf.

Leggy Tall and straggling growth caused by insufficient light.

Loam Friable soil mix made up of clay, sand and rotted leaves.

GLOSSARY

Margin The edge of a leaf or flower. Sometimes a different colour or shade than the rest of the leaf or flower.

Midrib The main vein of a leaf, which is often raised above the surface.

Offset A small plantlet formed at the base of the parent plant and can be detached and used for propagation.

Organic fertilizer Developed from a living source, for example, compost.

Perennial A plant that lives for three or more years under normal conditions.

Photosynthesis A process through which the leaves produce food from light, air and moisture.

Plantlet A young plant.

Pot-bound A plant that has filled its container with roots and will no longer develop without being repotted into a larger pot.

Propagate A means of producing new plants through cuttings or division.

Rest period A stage in the year when the plant becomes inactive and where there is little or no growth.

Rhizome A horizontal stem, usually underground, which stores food and water and produces new stems and roots.

Root The underground section of a plant, which absorbs food and moisture from the soil.

Rootball The mass of roots and potting soil that is seen when the plant is removed from its pot.

Rosette The circular arrangement of leaves growing from a central point.

Spadix A fleshy spike embedded with small flowers, usually surrounded by a spathe.

Spathe The large colourful bract surrounding the spadix.

Sphagnum moss Dried, water-retaining moss that can be incorporated in a potting soil mix and is usually used inside a moss stick.

Spike Closely arranged, stemless flowers on a single stem.

Spore The reproductive cell of a non-flowering plant.

Sub-tropical A plant originating from an area outside of the tropics, but is susceptible to the cold.

Succulent A plant that stores water in fleshy stems and leaves.

Tendril The thin, curling extension of a stem or leaf, which enables a plant to climb.

Tropical A plant that originates from an area between the tropics of Capricorn and Cancer.

Tuber Fleshy stems or roots that store food and water.

Undulate Having a wavy edge, usually of a leaf or petal margin.

Variegated Blotches or streaks of another colour found on flowers or leaves.

Whorl A circle of three or more leaves which grow from a single node.

INDEX

Illustrated pages are indicated in **bold**

PHOTOGRAPHIC CREDITS

Marianne Alexander: pages 13, 14–15, 26 (top, bottom right), 27, 24 (right), 25 (top left, bottom), 46 (bottom left, bottom right), 47 and 53.

Sheila Brandt: pages 12, 19, 20–21 and 26 (left).

Juan Espi: pages 10–11, 17, 28–29, 40 and 50–51.

Craig Fraser/SIL: Front cover (top centre, top right, bottom left, centre); half title; title; pages 4–5, 6, 18, 25 (right), 31, 36–37, 38, 41, 46 (top), 54, 106, 112 and back cover.

Nancy Gardiner: Front cover (top left, centre right, bottom centre, bottom right); front cover flap; spine; pages 24 (left), 30, 56–105 and back cover flap.

Paul Gordon/*House & Leisure*: page 34.

Francois Hancke: pages 8, 48–49 and 52.

Zelda Wahl: pages 39, 42, 43, 44 and 45.

SIL = Struik Image Library